Suicidal Women

THEIR THINKING AND FEELING PATTERNS

CHARLES NEURINGER

University of Kansas

and

DAN J. LETTIERI

National Institute on Drug Abuse

GARDNER PRESS, INC.
New York

COPYRIGHT © 1982 BY GARDNER PRESS, INC.

Gardner Press, Inc.
19 Union Square West
New York 10003

Library of Congress Cataloging in Publication Data

Neuringer, Charles, 1931-
  Suicidal women.

  Bibliography: p.
  Includes indexes.
  1. Women--United States--Suicidal behavior. I. Lettieri, Dan J. II. Title. (DNLM: 1. Suicide--Psychology.
2. Women--Psychology. HV 6546 N494s)
HV6546.N48   362.2   81-6294
ISBN 0-89876-023-2   AACR2

Printed in the United States of America

To

Edwin S. Shneidman

and

Norman L. Faberow

PREFACE

Suicide is the only "psychiatric" disorder that is lethal. According to the Bureau of Vital Statistics, there is one well-authenticated suicidal death every half-hour of every day. This grim statistic is based only on death certificates that have "suicide" entered as the mode of death. The actual rate has been calculated to be far greater than the official rate.

There has been a resurgence of interest in the problem of suicide during the last ten years. A special suicide study center was created at the National Institute of Mental Health. A national organization, the American Association of Suicidology, has been founded to help prevent suicide. Journals devoted to the problem of suicide and unpredicted deaths have come into being. These efforts have earned the study of suicide the special discipline title of *Suicidology*.

The interest in suicide is far older than suicidology. The ancient philosophers, the medieval theologians, and the scientists of the Enlightenment have tried to find a key to understanding of the nature of suicide. Modern sociological and psychiatric theorists have also tried to solve the puzzle of why some people choose death. The latter's effort has been directed toward trying to "tease out" the personality and motivational variables leading to suicidal decisions, but they have failed in this task. The search for personality structures and motivational dynamics associated with suicide has not borne fruit. Because of this failure the focus of suicidology has turned toward prevention through social engineering. Massive preventive "hygiene" efforts have been developed which it is hoped will reduce the suicide rate.

Two considerations guided the planning of our research. The first of these had to do with the role of cognitive factors in producing suicidal decisions and the second involved evaluating those cognitive strategies in self-destructive women.

It is the authors' contention that the key to suicide does not lie in the area of personality and motivational forces but is the product of the cognitive and intellectual organization of the suicidal individual. It is also our contention, based upon the research described in this volume (as well as on other investigations) that suicide is the result of a style of organizing experiences (i.e., some people use a particular thinking pattern that leads them irresistibly toward suicidal decisions). It is the manner in which people organize and interpret the world, and not the events themselves, that is the key to the appearance of self-destruction. What has emerged from our study is that there is a particular style of thinking described in this volume that leads some people to organize their experience in such a way that suicide is the only possible choice for them.

The authors feel that the data in this report advances a new direction for suicidology initially developed by Edwin S. Shneidman, an orientation which breaks with the traditional views of the etiology of suicide. We feel that traditional conceptualizations of the causes of suicide need to be reexamined if the suicide rate is to be reduced in ways other than on a hit-or-miss basis.

While the amount of research on all aspects of suicide has grown over the years, there exists an important area in this discipline which has been slighted for various non-anti-feminist reasons. Research on the suicidal behavior of females has not been one of the major concerns of suicidology. The research that has been done on female suicide has tended to be either statistical surveys or attempts to relate suicide to female physiology. Little or no work has been done on the cognitive and intellectual states of suicidal women.

Although three times fewer women kill themselves than do men, female attempters outnumber male attempters by three to one. Even though fewer women die by their own hands than do men, the female suicidal death rate is still alarming. An analysis of female suicide statistics tells us that one women dies by suicide every hour and a half. While the female rate may be "low" when compared to that of the males, the suicide-per-hour-clock ratio brings home the impact of the number of female suicide deaths. Each death is the story of a human tragedy. This situation is becoming increasingly frightening since recent vital statistics indicate that suicide is on the rise in general and is rising fastest among adolescent girls.

Suicidologists' unintentional slighting of female suicide is to some degree understandable. The very high suicide rate among men has captured suicidologists' attention and has created a greater sense of urgency than the lower female rate. In addition, there may be a historical reason for the focusing on male suicide. Because of recent wars, there exists a large pool of male suicidal patients residing in the Veterans Administration Hospital system. This large concentration has compelled the development of suicide research and prevention activities as well as making large-scale research projects feasible. It is no surprise that suicide research has historically been oriented toward males. However, with the increasing establishment of suicide-prevention agencies, we are becoming aware of the extent of suicidal behavior in women, and it is now possible to direct research efforts toward this group since women are the major clientele of these centers. Various commentators have in the past argued that female suicide is not a critical problem, but it may be that the extent of female suicidal behavior was being masked by the absence of such data-concentrating facilities.

We have already stated that we feel the study of the cognitive organization of suicidal thinking is the direction that will lead to great rewards in preventing suicide. The previous modest research carried out in this area has been conducted with male populations. Our study attempted to (1) expand our understanding of suicidal cognition and (2) to extend it to the thinking and feeling patterns of self-destructive women. There exist lacunae in suicide theory and research because our knowledge is based on only half of the human race. We hope that this study has redressed that imbalance.

All members of the mental health community are faced with having to make judgments about suicidal risks. With the expansion of the therapeutic community, more and more individuals are involved with the delivery of mental health services. Not only are the traditional professions (psychiatry, psychology, medicine, social work, and others) involved in dealing with suicidal problems, but now paraprofessionals (caseworkers, counselors, gatekeepers, and others) are faced with having to make decisions that affect men and women's lives. The data found in this volume should be of great interest and importance to anyone whose task is to predict if another human being will attempt to make an end of his existence.

The authors wish to express their gratitude to the many people and agencies who supported our research. We owe a great debt to the staff of the Los Angeles Suicide Prevention Center. They gave us space, encouragement, consultation, and their expertise. We would like specially to thank them for the time and effort they expended in making lethality ratings of our subjects. We would also like to express our appreciation to the staffs of the inpatient and outpatient ser-

vices of the University of California (Los Angeles) Medical
Center for providing facilities and access to their clients.

This research would not have been possible without a
preliminary seed grant made to the senior author by the
University of Kansas Biomedical Research Support Committee. That committee's encouragement allowed us to initiate
the research program. Sustaining support was provided by a
National Institute of Mental Health grant (No. MH 15103)
awarded to the senior author.

We also both wish to express our appreciation to Gardner
Spungin who had faith in this book, and most important,
had patience with our slow pace.

Finally, we wish to express our gratitude to all the
women who participated in this study. Many of them told us
that they wanted to help because they hoped that what we
were doing would benefit themselves and others.

Charles Neuringer
Lawrence, Kansas
Dan J. Lettieri
Washington, D.C.

CONTENTS

I

THE NATURE OF SUICIDE

Albert Camus, the French philosopher, once said that "There is but one truly serious philosophical problem, and that is suicide. Judging whether life is or is not worth living amounts to answering the fundamental question of philosophy. All the rest — whether or not the world has three dimensions, whether the mind has nine or twelve categories — comes afterwards." (1959, p. 3).

Philosophers have long grappled with the problem of suicide, but they examined and tried to understand it from the position of moral justification. From the pagan Stoics to the Church Fathers, philosophers agree that suicide was an attempt to withdraw or escape from life. The Stoics, especially Seneca, tell us that if a man finds life unbearable and if reason requires his death, suicide is justified. Cato, Brutus and Cassius were examples of stoical deaths. When life became oppressive, they chose not to live on in a degraded manner but to die. Socrates, Plato and Aristotle considered suicide a crime against the state but felt that it was justified in many cases (Landsberg, 1953).

According to Williams (1957) there was apparently no great taboo associated with suicide in the Greco-Roman world. However, the early Christian church philosophers condemned suicide. St. Augustine, deriving his view from the Ten Commandments, equated suicide with homicide. St. Thomas Aquinas believed suicide to be contrary to man's inclinations. Furthermore, he argued, since man is God's property, only divine judgment could make decisions about mortality. The belief that suicide was sinful developed to such a point that by the time of Dante's *Divine Comedy*, suicides were assigned to the seventh circle of Hell while Satan himself occupied the ninth and last circle. Modern philosophers such as Hume, Montesquieu, Fichte and Schopenhauer restated the humanist point of view that man was master of his own fate and could therefore make his own decisions about disposing of his life (Silving, 1957).

Within the last twenty years, the bulk of the literature on the psychology of suicide has addressed itself to the problems of epidemiological incidence, personality characteristics, identification and prediction through the use of psychological tests, and to prodromal behavioral clues to suicide. This last area is of major practical and rehabilitative importance in heading off and preventing suicide in hospital and clinical settings.

The history of science (Kuhn, 1962) suggests that in order for an area of study to obtain the status of a science it must employ at least one commonly accepted fundamental theoretical paradigm from which subsequent predictions can be derived and tested. Although a number of hypotheses have been suggested (Freud, 1922; Binswanger, 1958; Shneidman, 1963b; Naroll, 1961; Menninger, 1938; Henry & Short, 1954) to account for suicidal behavior, none has had overwhelming acceptance. It is reasonable to suggest that suicide research is in the preparadigm stage of scientific evolution.

This is not to imply that research has not been carried out in scientific fashion, but merely that much groundwork is still needed in view of the fact that no single theory has been found to account for all the multifarious aspects of suicide. As Shneidman (1963b) has pointed out, the problem is in part one of taxonomy and definition of suicidal behavior. Any nosologic scheme, to be experimentally heuristic, must on the one hand allow strict operational definitions and also be in a form general enough to allow modificaion and revisions. From a variety of such schemes to be found in the literature (Shneidman, 1963a; 1963b; McEvoy, 1963; Dublin, 1963; Neuringer, 1962), Shneidman's (1963b) scheme is perhaps the most comprehensive while McEvoy's (1963) scheme is the most operational.

SUICIDE AND INSANITY

One of the oldest issues in suicidology has focused on the phenomenon's standing along a normal-abnormal continuum. The relevance of the issue here is not so much whether one accepts suicidal behavior as psychopathological or not but rather the consequences of taking a polarized stand on the issue. Due to the early nineteenth-century view of suicide as a sign of insanity suicidology became the domain of physicians and psychologists. Not until later in the century when suicide was viewed as only occasionally the act of an insane individual were research avenues opened to sociological and biochemical investigators. The Oxford English Dictionary states that the word "suicide" was first used in English in 1651. Some etymologists note that the word "suicide" may have been derived from the words "suist" (meaning a selfish man) and/or "suicism" (meaning selfishness). Seventeenth-century law distinguished between *felo de se* (murder of self) and suicide. *Felo de se* referred to a self-destructive act by a mentally sound individual while suicide referred to a self-destructive act by a mentally unsound individual.

Although Falret (1822) contended that all suicides were insane, his list of causes of suicide could not be viewed as characteristic of the insane suicide exclusively. Esquirol (1838) and Brierre de Boismont (1865) began to question whether all suicides were insane. Lisle (1856) suggested that only one in four suicides were insane. In England, Westcott (1885) categorized three types of suicide in mentally sound individuals: (1) suicide due to a passion or rage; (2) suicide in such a mental state that the individual has no free choice (i.e., of two alternatives, suicide is the least odious); and (3) deliberate suicide (e.g., religious zealots, soldiers). In a sample of 52 nonpsychotic suicides, Brockhaus (1922) found all to be due to either a character anomaly or too narrow an outlook.

It was because of the mid-19th-century view that the causes of suicide might not reside solely in the individual (in particular, the insane individual) that broader social scientific approaches appeared. Morselli (1879) regarded suicide as a social fact, and felt that it was the result of the struggle for life and human selection. Reflecting a somewhat similar point of view Durkheim (1898) and Halbwachs (1930) suggested that many suicides were socially caused.

More recently, Bergler (1946) contended that all suicides were insane while Zilboorg (1936a, 1936b) and Pollack (1957) admitted that not all suicides need be insane. Stengel and Cook (1958) found 40% of their suicidal sample to be mentally disturbed; however, Cavan (1926); Dublin and Bunzel (1933); Piker (1938); Siewers and Davidoff (1943); Arieff et al., (1948); Stanton and Schwartz (1954); Farberow and Shneidman (1955); and Shneidman and Farberow (1957) found considerably smaller percentages of severely disturbed and psychotic individuals in their respective suicidal samples. One of the most recent studies (Weisz, et al., 1967) found the suicide-threatener and suicide-attempter groups to contain 13% and 12% psychotic individuals respectively. In a study of hospitalized schizophrenics Shneidman, Farberow and Leonard (1962) concluded that suicide was the result of planned and organized action.

In light of the equivocal findings in the above-cited research, it would appear that it is difficult to link suicide to psychosis in any definitive way.

PSYCHOLOGICAL THEORIES OF SUICIDE

Psychological theories have been developed to delineate those characteristics common to the suicidal as contrasted to the nonsuicidal personality. Two underlying themes characterize the bulk of these theories: (1) there exist various personality syndromes (clusters of personality variables) relatively unique to the suicidal individual; and (2) the determinants of suicidal behavior reside solely within the individual. While the influence of other people is recognized, the theories deal with these influences minimally or in terms of the suicidal person's images of others. In short, the theoretical focus is intrapersonal.

Psychoanalytic Theories

The underlying assumption in the Freudian approach is that of retroflexed rage; a person kills himself because he originally intended to kill someone else.

In his early work, Freud (1917) contended that the individual who loses someone he dearly loves — either because the loved one rejects him or the loved one dies — feels abandoned and this feeling of abandonment and rejection eventually swells up in the individual and he becomes angry. If the supposed abandoning person is no longer available and the anger cannot be directed against that individual, then the anger becomes directed against the individual's memory (his introject) of that person and the individual wants to kill the memory (i.e., hostility is turned inward — the inversion hypothesis). Regrettably, the attempt to kill a portion of one's memory is usually lethal. It is important to note that Freud was speaking about depression that eventually turns to anger and the desire to kill the person causing the hurt.

In his later work, Freud (1920), like Jung, grafted on to his theory some of the findings of physics. Both were impressed with the second law of thermodynamics. For Jung, the death experience was a way to growth — it was or could be a meaningful experience — however, for Freud, the death experience was only destructive. Freud postulated two basic instincts: Eros (the life instinct) and Thanatos (the death instinct). The death instinct accounted for aggressiveness and destructiveness in man. Freud went so far as to say that "the goal of all life is death " (1920, p. 38). Life then proceeds toward death, in part because all organic matter seeks to return to its original inorganic state.

Karl Menninger's (1938) suicide theory utilized the later Freudinan concepts of the life and death instincts. He emphasized the power of the Eros and Thanatos drives and conceived of them constantly struggling for dominance in the psyche of man. With Thanatos in ascendency, the individual becomes destructive and neurotic and, should Thanatos continue to dominate, the person may take his own life. Menninger's views have the "morality play" flavor of the battle between "good" and "evil." Dr. Menninger goes on to postulate the necessary presence of three psychic components before suicide can occur:

1. The wish to kill (sadism).
2. The wish to be killed (masochism).
3. The wish to die (submission).

In the wish to kill, primitive hostility and aggression, due to frustration, appear, and the individual may commit suicide as a means of punishing others. The wish to be killed is the wish to kill turned inward because of the guilt engendered by a harsh superego. The wish to die is interpreted as a submissive-passive giving up due to the overwhelming power of Thanatos.

Menninger also speculated on the symbolic meanings of the different modes of self-destruction. The passive person prefers ingesting poison or barbiturates. Tabachnick (1957) suggested that many patients who attempted suicide via barbiturate ingestion have had difficulties with their mothers and been rejected by them. He hypothesized that the barbiturate ingestion was a symbolic reingestion or winning back of the mother. Menninger theorized that dying by fire might symbolize a desire for warmth denied the depressed individual because of rejection. Drowning symbolized a return to the womb, and being run over by an automobile was a submissive act. Futterman (1961) considered suicide a manifestation of the conservatism of the death instinct and its attempt to maintain a status quo likened to a union with the breast.

Adler (1958) described the suicidal individual as one who tried to hurt others by hurting himself. Such a person is vain, narcissistic, expecting other people to think only of him, but when confronted with the truth, he reverts to the fantasied operation of hurting others by hurting himself. Ansbacher (1961) extended Adler's idea of control with the notion that the contemplation of suicide may give the individual a feeling of mastery. The act itself, however, is seen as one of hostility and reproach directed at those who did not supply nurturants to the suicidal individual.

The Sullivanian view as presented by Green (1961) interprets suicide as an attempt to coerce and beg from people. Horney's (c.f., DeRosis, 1961) approach to personality regards suicide as self-hatred erupting in a framework of self-alienation; a separation of the idealized self from the subjective self.

Bergler (1946) follows the Freudian psychoanalytic theory but implies that Introjection is not the only process that can lead to suicide. He discusses two other types of suicide: Hysterical Suicide and Superego Suicide. Hysterical Suicide is seen as an unconscious dramatization of how one does *not* want to be treated, accompanied by a childish misconception of death as lacking finality. Superego Suicide is to be found in paranoid schizophrenics, who project their superegos out into the world, and hear voices commanding them to kill themselves.

Most of the psychoanalytic theories broadly follow Freud's inversion hypothesis that outwardly directed hostility becomes transformed into inwardly directed hostility. The death instinct (Thanatos) may or may not be utilized. Jung intimates some sort of mystical rebirth experience, and Sullivan seems to be dealing more with the interpersonal manipulative aspects of suicide attempts and not the committing of the act.

Jungian Analytic Theories

In his earlier work Jung (1925) viewed suicide as a form of rebirth (or birth of a new cycle) which permitted the suicidal individual a fresh start. If this fresh start has religious tones, then the individual may commit suicide to reach a nirvana in which there is some guaranteed immortality, afterlife, or omnipotence. O'Connor (1948) emphasized the suicide's return to an earlier state of power-narcissism, a kind of immortal omnipotence. If the fresh start is not tinged with religious dogma (i.e., there is no expectation of a life after death), Jung would have argued that life preceding birth is to be preferred by the suicidal individual over the imbalance and tension so unresolvable in the present life. The struggle between the polarities of life vs. death becomes unbalanced in favor of death as a form of regression. The suicide achieves complete regression to non-life.

Followers of Jung, such as Hillman (1964) and Klopfer (1961) interpreted Jung to mean a return to the womb of the Magna Mater. In his later writings Jung (1953) became enchanted with the second law of thermodynamics, and he attempted to graft this physical law onto psychological theory. The law states briefly that organic (living) matter seeks to return to its original inorganic state. This idea is popularized in the adage "From dust to dust." In his global fashion, Jung was suggesting that the suicidal person might be trying to return to some original (inorganic) state.

Klopfer (1961) expanded on the rebirth theme and suggested that the nonfatal suicidal crisis can be a profoundly spiritual experience which gives a new meaning to life. Thus he seems to be saying what many war novelists have said — namely that the soldier who comes close to death comes away from such experiences with a new outlook on life, a new zest for life.

In another context, some researchers have recently studied fatal one-car accidents (Tabachnick, 1967; Tabachnick & Litman, 1966). They propose that such accidents are probably seldom random and that the driver may be seeking a different and better life.

A Potpourri of Paradigms

George A. Kelly (1961) viewed man as a completely rational being (he does not employ the notion of an unconscious). Man, in fact, is viewed as a kind of scientist. He has certain hunches about reality and, like the scientist, he accepts or rejects these on the basis of whether or not they are confirmed in reality.

Kelly argued that the suicidal act has different meanings for different individuals and to understand the act necessitates that we examine that individual's system of hunches or constructs about reality. Thus there are potentially as many different reasons for suicide as there are individuals who commit suicide. It is important to note that Kelly viewed the act of suicide as completely conscious, rational and idiosyncratic. Zilboorg (1936b) saw suicide as a way of thwarting outside forces that are making life impossible, pointing out the mystical, paradoxical aspects of suicide, which achieves living by killing the self. The suicide feels he can experience the effects of his death. People will mourn for him and feel sorrow over his demise. Through the one grand gesture of killing himself, he gains immortality, fame and maintains a kind of self-perpetuation. Zilboorg (1936a) had already noted the aura of infantile omnipotence surrounding this kind of magical thinking. Binswanger (1958) spoke of the suicide as an individual whose experience of the weight of the present cuts off all views of the future, one who feels oppressed by the "now" so that all exits are blocked. He is immobilized and sees no future for himself. The only road toward life is by some act. Suicide then becomes an attempt to affirm one's identity and existence. The act of making such a decision dissolves the weight of the present and therefore reaffirms existence. But where existence is affirmed by the relinquishing of life, there the existence is a tragic one.

Wahl (1957) saw suicide as the supreme act of hostility toward the world. Through magical thinking the suicide destroyed the whole world by obliterating it from his consciousness when he died. Bender and Schilder (1937) felt that spite is important and emphasized again the stress on suicide as an act of hostility. The suicide punished people in order to extort extra love. Bender and Schilder spoke mostly of children where the differences between life and death are not too clearly understood. They also asserted that developmental anomalies and abnormalities are a predisposing factors in suicide.

With the exception of Binswanger and Kelly's work, hostility plays a great role in the psychological as well as the psychoanalytic theories. Unfortunately, we do not know if the hostility is in the suicidal individual or in the survivors who gratuitously assign it to the suicide. Hostility may certainly be found in suicide notes (Shneidman & Farberow, 1957), but so are many other things. Present personality theories have difficulty in clearly explaining why suicides occurred *instead* of something else.

There is a limited but growing literature (Ansbacher, 1961; Breed, 1967; Farberow, 1962a, 1962b; Peck, 1965, 1968; Sullivan, 1956) which focuses on the interpersonal lifestyle of the suicidal individual. The underlying tenet of such approaches has been that the suicidal act is a coping or adaptive process in response to overwhelming feelings of powerlessness and hopelessness.

Appelbaum (1963) contends that the suicidal individual views the suicidal act as an appropriate coping technique in the face of feelings of extreme distress and powerlessness.

The suicidal person sees his past as a time when things were better, his present as a time of helplessness, and his future as a time when things will not get any better. Partly a function of his narrow, restricted viewpoint, the potential suicide sees no alternative other than suicide.

A related avenue of research (Leonard, 1967; Hendin, 1964; Read, 1936) has stressed the early interpersonal interactions the child has experienced. It is these early learned coping tactics which theorists suggest are the singularly important influences that may dispose the individual to suicide in later life.

BIOLOGICAL THEORIES OF SUICIDE

Sainsbury's study (1966) of suicides in London found that 10 out of 390 suicides had physical deformities. Dorpat and Ripley (1960) found some support for the notion that self-destructive tendencies may lead to tissue destruction as evidenced by the high frequency of physical disorders in their sample of completed suicides. LeShan (1962) found high correlations between cancer and suicide but did not venture an explanation of the correlation. Schmale (1958) hypothesized that feelings of hopelessness or helplessness are related to (or may result in) increased biological vulneralibility and disease.

A resurgence of interest in biochemical factors in suicide is currently focused on urinary analyses (Bunney & Fawcett, 1965, 1967). The results are interesting, but only highly suggestive at this stage of research.

SOCIOLOGICAL THEORIES OF SUICIDE

A number of theorists (Durkheim, 1951; Porterfield, 1949; Powell, 1958; Naroll, 1961; Gibbs & Martin, 1964; and

Henry & Short, 1954) have focused on the importance of certain sociological variables (status-integration, economic depressions, status mobility, rural vs. urban habitat, seasonal fluctuations, etc.) rather than psychological variables.

Durkheim

Many good things seem to go with high status: greater income, more possessions, increased travel, less likelihood of psychosis, longer life, etc. There is, however, one risk accompanying high status that may reconcile some to a position short of the top — the possibility of suicide is greater there. In 1879, Durkheim (1951) commented that the possessors of most comfort suffer most. Durkheim's work was done by a thorough examination of statistical records. He sought correlations between suicide rates and the rates of various social factors such as marriage, divorce, occupation, religion, etc. In his classic work, *Suicide: A Sociological Study*, Durkheim conceived of suicide as a function of three major social factors, which in turn describe his three basic types of suicide:

1. Altruistic suicide is characterized by high social cohesion, dogmatic acceptance of the goals of society and an overintegration with society.
2. Egoistic suicide is characterized by high social diffusion, low group solidarity, and a lack of integration with society; in short, a loosely knit society in which the individual can find little restraint.
3. Anomic (normless) suicide is depicted as a breakdown of the individual's guidelines and norms within the social system such as might occur during economic depressions, divorce proceedings, etc.

Henry and Short

Two contemporary sociologists, Henry and Short (1954), have expanded and updated much of Durkheim's original work. They proposed that (1) rates of suicide are higher where there are the highest socioeconomic statuses, and (2) suicide rates are higher for those individuals who have little close involvement with other persons as compared with the rates for those who have much involvement. Statistical evidence tends to support their postulates. For example, it has been found that suicide rates are higher in the centers of large urban cities than in rural areas (Schmid, 1928; Cavan, 1926). In these urban areas one finds among other things rooming houses and cheap apartment hotels in which the inhabitants are often anonymous, isolated, homeless people. It has also been found that single individuals have higher suicide rates than married individuals. Henry and Short suggest that married people have at least one meaningful involvement, while single individuals probably do not. In summary, Henry and Short view suicide as the plague of high status and social isolation.

A few sociologists have examined the relationship of socioeconomic status to suicide more closely (Yap, 1958; Sainsbury, 1956) and have shown that the suicide rate is also relatively high in the lower-status group. In particular, Breed (1963) argues that it is not high status per se that is related to increased suicide rates, but that suicidal individuals at the time of death in a New Orleans sample were downwardly mobile. In effect, Breed contends that this downward mobility (moving from a higher to a lower socioeconomic status) may be the relevant factor for suicide.

In later formations, Henry and Short combined their two basic postulates into one and called it "freedom from external restraint." Put simply, people who are involved in many solitary relationships must frequently act so as to meet the expectations and wishes of other people. The connection between high status and social isolation is instanced in the high-status individual who must singly make all decisions and bear the full weight and responsibility of such decisions. It is in this respect that he has no "external restraints."

If we examine this problem closely, one must ask why the risk of suicide increases with the increases in personal freedom. Fromm (1941), a humanist with wide-ranging interests, proposed that the dilemma of modern man is that he wants independence, yet seeks to escape from freedom. Fromm argued that man cannot at this point in evolution tolerate complete freedom from external restraints. Man needs limits and restraints that may serve as clear objects on which he can direct and ventilate his frustrations.

AN INTERESTING OMISSION

The major theoreticians of suicide have without exception made no differentiation between the sexes concerning the psychodynamics of suicide. They appear to hold general views that apply to both men and women. Their implicit assumption seems to be that motives and suicidal adaption apply equally for both sexes and that all human beings are equal victims before the laws of suicide. While there seem to be no differences between men and women as far as the dynamics of suicide, there are differences in the expression of the suicidal urge by the sexes. The way in which women display their suicidal behavior is examined in the next chapter.

II

SUICIDAL BEHAVIOR IN FEMALES

Because women kill themselves less often than men, Dublin (1963) has called suicide a masculine behavior. While women do not take their own lives as often as men, they tend to threaten and attempt suicide at a higher rate than males. The differential suicide death rates for men and women are impressive (Robins et al., 1959; Shneidman & Farberow, 1961; Stengle, 1964; Davis, 1968). This differential exists regardless of age, race, or marital status. The gap between the number of male and female suicides increases with age. At the 20–25-year-old range, the ratio of male to female suicides is approximately 2 to 1. At the 60-year-old level, the ratio has widened to 10 to 1 (Johnson, 1979). Differences in the methods of suicide used by men and women also exist. Men tend to use the more violent methods, (e.g., firearms, jumping, and hanging). Women use less violent methods such as barbiturate or poison ingestion (Lester, 1972; Davis, 1967; Dublin, 1963; Lester & Lester, 1971; Maris, 1969; Marks & Abernathy, 1974; Marks & Stokes, 1976).

The sex differentials are reversed for suicide attempts. Women predominate over men in this type of suicidal behavior. However, suicide-attempt men still tend to utilize the more violent suicidal methods and women the less lethal methods (Rubenstein et al., 1958; Dorpat & Boswell, 1963; Hendin, 1950; Maris, 1969; Lendrum, 1933; Phillips & Muzaffer, 1961).

Regardless of whether or not the suicide attempt is successful, suicidal males tend to be older than the females by about 5 to 10 years (Davis, 1968). Female suicide attempters tend to be diagnosed as neurotics or affect disorders more often than the men. The males are generally described as either schizophrenic or psychopathic (Lester, 1972).

Since 3 or 4 times as many women attempt suicide than men, it is no surprise that they make up the bulk of client populations contacting suicide prevention facilities (Heilig, 1968). More disturbing is the report that young girls comprise 90% of all adolescent suicide attempts (Cantor, 1972).

In 1897, when Durkheim finished his historic study of suicide, he announced that femininity was a protection against suicide (1951). There are three major questions about female suicidal behavior. They are: (1) Why do fewer females commit suicide than do males? (2) Why do more women attempt suicide than men? (3) What motivates those women who successfully kill themselves? Answers to the first two questions may be roughly categorized as either "physiological," or "social role" explanations. As seen in the previous chapter, the personality-oriented theories of suicide are strangely silent on the subject of sex differences in suicide. That silence seems to be due to their taking the position that the psychodynamics of suicide apply equally to men and women.

PHYSIOLOGICAL FACTORS

The attributing of sex role differentials in suicidal behavior to biological or physiological differences between men and women has led various theorists to diverse conclusions. Lester (1972) attributes women's low suicide death rate to their small and fragile musculature i.e., they are not "strong" enough to use the violent and therefore lethal methods of self-destruction. The menstrual cycle has been studied closely in terms of its relationship to suicidal behavior. Several studies have indicated that suicide attempt activity tends to occur most often either during the immediate premenstrual, menstrual, or postmenstrual phase of the cycle (Tonks, Rack & Rose, 1968; Dalton, 1959; Trautman, 1961; Wetzel & McClure, 1973; Mandell & Mandell, 1967). MacKinnon and MacKinnon (1956), utilizing autopsy evidence from successful suicide attempters, reported that most female self-destroyers were in the midleuteal phase. There is strong evidence for a connection between the menstrual cycle and suicide; most suicide attempts occur during the bleeding stage while most committed suicides occur during the ovulation phase.

There is little doubt that a menstrual cycle–suicide relationship exists. What is not understood is how the menstrual cycle actually influences suicidal behavior. Smith (1975) reports that approximately one third of *all* women report negative affect changes during menstruation with the most prominent complaint being that of "irritability." It could be that the negative affect change, along with the "messiness" and "cramps" of menstruation, may be just one more irritant to an already overburdened and failing personality organization (i.e., "the last straw"). To a woman having adaptational difficulties, menstruation may be an added stress that finally disrupts a tenuous hold on life. As such it may act as any general stressor which further weakens a deteriorating personality organization. On the other hand, menstruation may have a particular psychological meaning to some women (e.g., a sign of weakness, defenselessness, helplessness or passivity).

For some it may be an unwanted reminder of femininity, especially for those women who are ambivalent about their female status. Whether menstruation is conceived of as a general or a particular stressor, it may combine with failing ego defenses to produce a disgust with oneself and life in general.

There have been speculations that the hormonal changes accompanying menstruation may be instrumental in causing suicidal behavior. Some women have inherited endocrine abnormalities, and these abnormalities may trigger severe psychological depressions. Suicide may thus be the outcome of these endocrine abnormalities (Winston, 1969; Dewhurst, 1968). However, the evidence for this hypothesis is extremely equivocal.

No adequate explanation of the relationship between committed suicide and ovulation has been offered.

Pregnancy has also been a factor that has been studied a great deal in terms of its effect on suicide. Surveys have indicated that suicidal behavior is a rare event in pregnant women (Rosenberg & Silver, 1965; Resnik, 1971; Sim, 1963; Whitlock & Edwards, 1968). The incidence of pregnancy in suicidal women varies from between 2 to 5 percent, which is below the pregnancy incidence in the general population. This proportion holds for both attempted and successful suicides. Barno (1967) states categorically that pregnancy is a protection against suicidal death.

Questions arise as to why pregnancy is considered a protection against suicide. If it truly is a deterrent, what has occurred in those women who have defied the pregnancy-suicide-deterrent hypothesis? There is no really persuasive argument as to why pregnancy should inhibit suicidal behavior. There may be endocrinological factors, such as the cessation of menstruation. This cessation may eliminate the effects of hormonal abnormalities or remove menstrual irritants. It may also be that seriously suicidal women feel the pregnancy will act as a solution to personal problems. Naive folklore holds that the coming of a baby will resolve difficulties with a husband or a lover. This usually turns out to be a deception, and the baby adds greater difficulties to the women's already overburdened coping mechanism. It is also possible that the low suicide rate among pregnant women may be due to scruples about destroying the foetus's life along with the mother.

What occurs in pregnant women who do commit suicide? There is very little data about successfully suicidal pregnant women. Goodwin and Harris (1979) indicate that suicide tends to occur mostly in the last two trimesters, whereas Rosenberg and Silver (1965) reported that most suicides occur during the first two trimesters. Rosenberg and Silver, as well as Whitlock and Edwards (1968), reported that more than half of the women were unmarried, implying guilt and shame were motivators toward the suicidal activity. On the other hand, Goodwin and Harris report that all of their sample were married. Goodwin and Harris attempted to tease out the social stress variables associated with the self-destructive behaviors. They report that in their sample the bulk of the women used violent methods and killed themselves in the home immediately following an argument with their husbands.

Goodwin and Harris speculate that pregnancy is perceived by some women as an entrapment, a loss of independence, a confirmation of their helplessness. Suicide occurs during the latter trimesters because at this time the woman is becoming more aware of the foetus. Stern (1968) offers an alternative hypothesis as to why pregnant women kill themselves: he feels that pregnant women are displacing their hostility from a husband or lover on to the foetus. They are symbolically killing the husband or lover and die only an incidental effect of this activity.

SOCIAL ROLE FACTORS

Various social role hypotheses have been put forward to explain the sex differentials in suicidal behaviors. Durkheim

(1951) ascribed the lower suicide rate in women to their lack of intellectual concern and unquestioning acceptance of traditional values. He claimed that women are not imaginative enough to commit suicide. Davis (1904) suggested that the suicide sex differences could be explained by the "naturally stronger religious faith of women." He did not explain why this "strength" does not act as a deterrent to suicidal attempts. Henry and Short (1954) feel that suicide is related to the business cycle, and that since women are less connected to this cycle than men, they will be less suicidal than men, and their high suicide attempt rate may be seen as a product of their failure to organize themselves well enough to successfully carry out the act. Maris (1969) and Lester (1972) have taken the position that women are less suicidal than men because they use the less violent and lethal method, and are consequently going to survive more often than the suicidal males. Diggory and Rothman (1961) implied that women are more vain than men and therefore eschew the more violent suicidal methods because they are disfiguring. Due to this vanity, women have a high survival rate. Marks and Abernathy (1974) and Marks and Stokes (1976) say that women use less violent suicidal methods because they are not acquainted with the operation of guns, ropes, and other traditionally male paraphenalia. Hamblin and Jacobson (1972) argue that disturbed women turn to drug abuse more often than disturbed men. They feel that drug abuse is a protective substitute for suicide. Sims (1974) feels that the higher use of legally prescribed drugs by women serves the same purpose.

Other than the possibility that the higher suicide attempt rate among women, as compared to men, is the result of failure to successfully commit suicide, there are some suggestions that women tend — more than men — to use suicide attempts as an aggression manipulation. Stengle (1964) hypothesizes that women are more manipulative than men and that they use suicidal gestures as a way of expressing aggression. Berkowitz (1962) also feels that aggression plays a role in female suicide. However, he ascribes the lower suicide rate in women to their being less aggressive than men. The attempted suicide is seen as behavior lower on the aggression-expression scale than committed suicide. Maris (1969) feels that since women are generally less isolated than men, they can more easily discharge their aggression in areas other than on themselves. Clifton and Lee (1976) see the expression of aggression as a problem of socialization; women are less confident and assertive than men and therefore tend to accept the blows of life more readily than men. Men's greater assertiveness leads them to express their aggression via suicide.

Two recent studies are of great interest. In one of these, Cantor (1972) ties suicidal behavior to sibling position in women. She reports that 84% of adolescent suicidal girls are either the first born or an only child in their family. This sibling position preponderance does not occur for suicidal boys. The implications of this study are not clear, but it does appear that ordinal position in the family may have a greater impact on women than men. A study by Taylor and Wicks (1980) has raised questions about the relationship between sex and suicidal method. Previous data (described above), has implied that women use less lethal methods than men regardless of whether the suicide is successful or not. These authors present compelling evidence that this relationship may not hold when racial and geographic variables are taken into consideration. Close examination of their data reveals various oddities in the relationship between sex and method. They report the existence of racial and regional differences among suicidal women. Sixty percent of the women killing themselves in Phoenix use guns (a "masculine" way of suicide). However, half of the female suicides in Cleveland use poison. Black female suicides use guns more often than white women in all major cities except Phoenix. The relationship between method and sex may be more complicated than heretofore thought.

One last point needs to be made about suicide-sex differentials. It is possible that this relationship may be an artifact of under-reporting of female suicidal activity. The public's general belief that women do not kill themselves may unconsciously influence coroner and medical examiners' decisions about the cause of death in the case of women.

It is now possible to offer some tentative answers to the three questions posed at the beginning of this chapter.

(1) *Why do fewer females commit suicide than males?* The differential may be due to the greater pressures associated with the male role in this society. Expectations about material accomplishment, sexual and athletic prowess may be experienced as exceptional burdens on males who are already having difficulties in coping. The socially defined female role probably allows disturbed women to escape from at least these demands. This differential expectation burden may disappear as more women are pressured into moving into managerial and professional roles.

(2) *Why do more women attempt suicide than men?* The answer to this question is also tied to sex-role expectation. Women have more resources than men for confessing their emotional difficulties. Men are expected to be strong, stolid, and not to publicly express their weaknesses. Women have covert approval to declare and display their perturbations and suicidal "display" is one of these socially sanctioned emotional outlets for disturbed women. In our society, dramatic and "hysterical" gestures and emotional displays are more acceptable in women than men. It may be that suicidal gestures are an expected, and even socially sanctioned, behavior in unhappy women. Their attempts certainly receive less disapproval than similar behavior in men. It is possible that suicide-attempt behavior is greatest in those disturbed women who have strong rigid and conventional sex role orientations.

(3) *What motivates women who successfully kill themselves?* Women who die by their own hand probably kill themselves for the same reasons as men do (i.e.,

despair, hopelessness, guilt, self-loathing, pain, remorse, fear, rage, and other negative emotions or conditions).

Sexual equality may well turn out to be a double-edged sword. While the advantages associated with equality (money, power, influence, achievement, etc.) certainly make striving for parity worthwhile, the disadvantages bring with it the darker aspects associated with the male role. Suicide can become an equal-opportunity death.

SUICIDAL THINKING

The hypothesis that the cognitive organizations of suicidal individuals are an important precurser to self-destructive behavior has a great attraction for many suicidologists. This insight was first voiced by Edwin S. Shneidman (1957, 1960, 1961) and was taken up by others (Beck, 1963; Neuringer, 1961, 1964a, 1964b, 1967, 1968, 1979a, 1979b). The promise of a cognitive clue to the nature of suicide is very exciting since motivational constructs have not proved to be very fruitful in leading to a comprehensive understanding of the nature of suicide. Direct relationships between motivational patterns and behavioral syndromes are highly elusive (and perhaps nonexistent). Motivational variables such as "sex identity confusion," "poor ego controls,"

25

"low frustration tolerance," and others seem to be etiological to a vast variety of pathological behavior. There do not seem to be any established relationships between particular personality characteristics and particular outcome behaviors. The closest psychology has ever come to that condition was in the early psychoanalytic writings and investigations of the etiology of certain psychosomatic disorders. However, later research has cast considerable doubt on the relationships envisaged by the psychoanalysts. To the practicing clinician, case histories and psychological reports begin to sound pretty much the same.

It may well be that both motivational dynamics and environmental stresses are universal, but people's perception of and reaction to these factors differ with each individual case. Behavioral consequences to similar stress situations vary quite extensively (i.e., some people grit their teeth and carry on, some give way to tears, some become schizophrenic and some become suicidal).

Following Shneidman's lead, the cognitively oriented suicidologists suggest that the manner in which life's experiences and conditions are perceived, coded, organized and understood is the basic clue to the explanation of why a suicidal "decision" is made. The primary question for suicidology is: What is there about how a person sees his world that leads him to want to abandon it?

The whole field of suicidology seems to be moving toward an emphasis on prevention rather than understanding (Shneidman, 1967). This movement reflects trends found in many mental health activities and is probably the outcome of the equivocal data and cul-de-sacs that have resulted from the failures associated with personality- and motivational-dominated research in suicide. On the other hand, some consistent progress has already been made in identifying cognitive variables directly related to suicidal behavior. There is now available evidence that dichotomous thinking (the tendency to think in bipolar opposites), a concept first introduced by Shneidman (1957, 1961) and elaborated upon by Neuringer (1961, 1967, 1968) is a large component of the thinking of suicidal individuals. Dichotomous thinking has also been found by Beck (1963) to exist in severely depressed persons. Rigidity (Neuringer, 1964a) and lability of thinking in suicidal persons (Neuringer, 1964b) has also been empirically demonstrated. It has also been established that a person's attitudes toward life and death are an important clue to suicidal behavior (Neuringer, 1961, 1967, 1968, 1979a). Of particular interest is the finding that the more clearly attitudes to life and death are juxtaposed (i.e., seen as separate and clear alternatives), the greater the suicidal danger (Neuringer, 1968, 1979b).

In general, the cognitive approach seeks to delineate the meaning of the suicidal act for the individual and how that meaning developed from particular intellectual styles.

Five avenues of investigation have been used toward achieving this goal. They are: (1) general thought processes as displayed in suicide notes; (2) confused or fallacious logic; (3) rigid, inflexible thinking; (4) narrow and dichotomous thinking; (5) and attitudes toward life and death.

SUICIDE NOTES

The notes left by suicides constitute a valuable and unusual data source concerning the ideation and affect of the suicidal person — particularly because they are often written a few moments before the individual kills his or her self and sometimes written as the individual is dying. Surprisingly, the formal study of suicide notes is a relatively new development which came about in the mid-1950s. It should be noted that only about 15% of the completed suicide population leave notes, and questions remain as to the comparibility of the note-writers and the non-note-writers. Shneidman and Farberow (1960) show evidence that the note-writers are not different from the non–note-writers in terms of age, sex, marital status or socioeconomic status. While this may be true, the question remains as to whether these sociological variables are the appropriate parameters to examine. One can argue that a dimension such as the need to communicate might be the appropriate or psychologically meaningful parameter which needs to be examined and controlled.

Farberow and Shneidman (1957) used notes as the basic data in an exploratory investigation of suicidal motivations over varying age groups. Utilizing Menninger's (1938) threefold suicidal motivation scheme, Farberow and Shneidman classified each note in one of the following four classes: wish to kill, wish to be killed, wish to die and unclassifiable. The primary finding was that for both sexes the wish to kill and the wish to be killed decreased with age. The findings must be interpreted cautiously in light of the fact that approximately 20% of the notes were unclassifiable. In a second study Shneidman and Farberow (1957) compared genuine and simulated suicide notes in terms of Mowrer's concepts of discomfort and relief. Mowrer's discomfort-relief content analysis technique divides any content into thought units that are scored for their qualities of discomfort, relief, or neutrality. The results of this study indicated that genuine note-writers were significantly more verbose, expressed significantly more discomfitures and displayed a significantly greater number of neutral statements. It was found, however, that neither the genuine nor the simulated notes contained much relief. Shneidman and Farberow interpreted the larger number of neutral states (which were primarily orders to be carried out) by the genuine note-writer as an indication of "an unrealistic feeling of omnipotence and omnipresence on the part of the suicidal individual" (1957, p. 255). The authors argued that it was possible for the suicidal person to think simultaneously (and contradictorally) of killing his or herself and of giving orders as though he or she would still be present to enforce them.

Tuckman, Kleiner and Lavell (1959) also examined the emotional content of suicide notes. They found that 51% of the notes displayed positive affect, such as gratitude and affection; 24% exhibited hostile or negative feelings and

25% were completely neutral in affect. The findings significantly indicated that persons aged 45 and over showed both
less affect and more neutral feelings than those under 45.
These authors regarded the high incidence of positive and
neutral affect as offering a more promising outlook for therapeutic intervention in potential suicides.

A study by Darbonne (1963) confirmed the previous
findings that neutral affect increased with age in a population
of suicide-note-writers. Darbonne's major conclusion was
that suicidal behavior is a symptom of various kinds of personality disorganization and not the result of a single suicidal
personality syndrome. This conclusion was based on his finding that the type of suicidal ideation and reasons offered for
the act varied according to the age of the suicidal person.

Shneidman and Farberow (1960) employed a very thorough content analytic methodology on 948 suicide notes
from the Los Angeles area. The importance of this study was
its sociopsychological and linguistic view, adopted from pro-
cedures developed by Osgood and Walker (1959), as well as
its sociological and ecological approach. In particular, the
authors found that by interrelating note-writers' ecological
habitats (on a continuum from most-advantaged suburbs to
least-advantaged apartment areas) with the reasons for the
suicide, as well as the affect expressed in the note, differences
were found among various ecological areas and the content of
the note. They concluded that suicide is neither the exclusive
domain of the psyche nor of the society, but is an admixture
of the two.

Spiegel and Neuringer (1963) tested the hypothesis that
a necessary condition for suicidal action is an inhibition of
the experience of dread originally evoked by suicidal intention. Using 33 pairs of matched genuine and simulated suicide
notes, the researchers found that genuine notes expressed
less suicidal intention, less suicide synonyms, were more
disorganized and had more instructions to the reader than
simulated notes. They concluded that just prior to suicidal
behavior, the suicide's attention is diverted from the behavior's
potentially dread-inducing negative qualities.

CONFUSED OR FALLACIOUS LOGIC

Shneidman (1957) has offered a lucid analysis of the sorts of logic and logical fallacies that suicidal individuals seem to employ. Of particular interest is Shneidman's notion of catalogical errors wherein the individual confuses the meaning of the self as experienced by the self with the meaning of the self as experienced by others. For example, the following argument, although deductively sound, confuses the meaning of the self (i.e., the error lies in the various conceptions of the pronoun "I"): "If anybody kills himself, then he will get attention; I will kill myself, therefore I will get attention."

RIGIDITY AND INFLEXIBILITY OF THOUGHT

An early study of 500 suicides led Muhl (1927) to conclude that suicide occurred in individuals who were not able to adjust to the demands of a changing environment. Williams (1936) reached a similar conclusion concerning the apparent inflexibility of the suicidal person. Neuringer (1964a) evaluated the question of whether rigid, inflexible thinking is a distinctive characteristic of suicidal individuals. He concluded that suicidal individuals displayed greater rigidity in thinking than two other nonsuicidal groups.

NARROW AND DICHOTOMOUS THINKING

There is a relatively long history to the observation that suicidal individuals display a narrow, highly focused and fixed thinking style. Westcott (1885) first observed the suicidal situation as one in which the person perceived only two odious alternatives, of which the least odious was suicide.

Brockhaus (1922) characterized suicide as due essentially to either a character anomaly or to too narrow an outlook. Cavan (1926) described the suicidal quality of "fixity of idea." Farrar (1951) remarked that suicidal persons had "gun-barrel vision." A variety of terms (e.g., "psychological myopia") have been employed by various authors (Farberow, 1962a; Shneidman, 1957, 1960; Appelbaum, 1963) to describe this characteristic thinking style.

Several studies put the oft-cited observation to an experimental test. A study by Neuringer (1961) on dichotomous thinking in suicidal individuals posed the question whether dichotomous thinking was a distinguishing characteristic of suicidal individuals. Three groups of patients were used: (1) suicide attempters; (2) nonsuicidal psychosomatic subjects; and (3) normal control patients. Neuringer had participants rate various concepts (e.g., life, death, suicide) on the evaluative factor of Osgood's Semantic Differential Scale (1957). His findings indicated that suicidal patients rated concepts significantly more dichotomously than the normal control patients but not appreciably greater than the psychomatic ones. Neuringer concluded at that time that dichotomous evaluative thinking seemed to be a common characteristic of emotionally disturbed individuals and not a factor exclusive to the thinking of suicidal persons. In a subsequent study Neuringer (1967) did find suicidal attempters more dichotomous on the activity and potency factors of the semantic differential than the nonsuicidal psychosomatic and normal control groups. Later studies that used a more sophisticated methodology demonstrated the presence of excessive dichotomous thinking in severely suicidal individuals (Neuringer, 1968, 1979a). In these studies, the suicidal patients were ranked in order of seriousness rather than treated as a homogeneous group. When the lethality of intention to die was taken into consideration, it became apparent that seriously suicidal persons think more dichotomously than non-seriously suicidal individuals and nonsuicidal persons.

ATTITUDES TOWARD LIFE AND DEATH

In a series of studies Neuringer (1961, 1967, 1968, 1979b) has established that the organization of attitudes toward life and death are related to level of suicidal activity. An early study (1961) compared an omnibus group of suicidal patients with psychosomatic and normal patients in terms of their attitude toward life and death. No significant differences were found. With more refined methodology (i.e., using only severely suicidal individuals) comparisons with other nonsuicidal but psychiatrically disturbed patients yielded data which indicated that suicidal individuals tend to devalue life more and fear death less than other people (1967, 1968). He also discovered that among suicidal individuals, the most severely self-destructive individuals see death as a state of positive attraction, and life as a negative state of being (1979a). He concluded that the common assumption that death is attractive and life unattractive is true only for the seriously suicidal person. It is this group out of all levels of suicidality which is truly committed to carrying out their self-demise. Other individuals on the suicidal continuum are mainly concerned with manipulation of others and have little interest in dying.

There is one final line of cognitive research which suggests that there may be a pattern of cognitive change leading up to and/or following the stressful suicidal episode. Farberow (1950) found less agitation and disturbance in suicide attempters than in threateners and suggested that this may have been the result of the attempt's tension-easing quality. Neuringer (1968) posed the same argument in explaining the attitudinal divergency data gathered from suicidal attempters. In a study on interpersonal relations Neuringer (1964b) concluded that "suicide may be another facet of the multitude of complex reactions that accompany cognitive changes under stress. . . . It is suggested that self-destructive behavior can be better understood as one of the many possible outcomes of cognitive change under stress" (pp. 54–55). Neuringer notes that Arieti (1955), Goldstein (1947) and

Hanfmann and Kasanin (1942) have suggested that anxiety may lead to reorganizations from greater to lesser cognitive differentiation. What is germane here is the notion of abreaction or patterned change in the suicide attempter following the attempt. It is not unreasonable to speculate that a similar abreaction may occur in the suicide threatener once he has voiced his threat and it has been heard. Therapeutically, the delineation of an abreactive state is important since it has been suggested that suicidal-attempt patients may appear hypernormal in the hopes of hastening release from the hospital and therapeutic care. If an abreaction effect can be empirically measured and/or instanced in terms of cognitive evaluations and changes in these evaluations over a period of time, a worthwhile diagnostic tool may be at hand.

It should be pointed out that the bulk of suicidal cognitive style research, cited above, has been conducted with males and generalized to all suicidal persons. This is due to the fact that there are more male than female suicide deaths and that materials pertaining to male suicides are therefore more available than for self-destructive females. Even though female suicide attempters outnumber male attempters, they are not as readily identified or taken as seriously as their male counterparts. In addition, this generalizing tendency has prevailed due to an assumption that the intellect of women does not essentially differ from that of men (i.e., men and women think the same way because they are of the same species). The objects of thought and the goals of the intellect may differ between the sexes, but the mediating thought processes themselves are biologically identical.

IV

BACKGROUND OF THE RESEARCH

A review of the literature indicates that while researchers have studied suicide attempters and completers, few have addressed themselves to an examination of the suicide threatener population. Present research has focused on suicide threateners. Specifically, four groups (varying in suicidal potential) were investigated in terms of (1) attitudinal, cognitive and affective states; (2) interrelationships among these states; and (3) patterns of changes in these states following the onset of the suicidal episode.

There are various reasons for the need of suicide research: (1) suicide is a serious mental health problem; (2) it has been relatively ignored as a research area, in part because of its taboo nature; (3) research has all too often relied on a posteriori interpretation, anecdotal case histories, infrequent direct tests of commonly accepted basic assumptions and a narrow focusing on residual data such as suicide notes, diaries, memories of friends and relatives; (4) a preponderance of attention on the smaller subpopulation of completed suicides rather than on the larger population of suicide threateners; and (5) a paucity of empirical work has looked at the attitudinal, affective and cognitive characteristics that may be necessary and/or sufficient determinants for a suicidal choice.

A conservative prediction of the number of suicides to be recorded in 1981 in the United States alone would be 23,000 (Dublin, 1963; Meerloo, 1962). In addition to this number, Shneidman and Farberow (1961) estimated that 7 to 8 times that number of individuals attempt suicide unsuccessfully each year. Dublin (1963) suggests that close to 2,000,000 people now living in the United States have a history of at least 1 suicidal attempt. If we add to these figures the unknown number of persons who may think or threaten suicide, but neither attempt nor commit it, the point to be made is clear: suicide is a serious mental health problem meriting scientific study.

The bulk of research within the last decade has addressed itself to the problems of epidemiological incidence, personality characteristics, prodromal behavioral clues and to identification and prediction through the use of psychological tests. The basic dilemma for research on completed suicides has been likened to the task of a coroner trying to perform an autopsy without a corpse. A notable attempt to deal with this problem has been made via the innovation of the psychological autopsy (Davis and Spelman, 1968; Shneidman, 1969; Curphey, 1961, 1967; Litman, 1968).

It would seem that researchers have directed much attention to the deceased suicidal individual at the regrettable cost of ignoring the living, potential suicide, viz., the suicide threatener. While it can be argued that study of completed suicides is scientifically laudable and of basic theoretical interest, the inherent methodological difficulties, as well as the temporal inapplicability for therapeutic intervention and prevention would suggest that investigative directions might be better served at the current preparadigmatic state of suicidology if focus were shifted to the potential suicidal individual who has not yet enacted self-destruction.

In this regard, it can be contended that the sine qua non for research must rest with the factors that effect a suicidal choice. In particular, it is believed that the attitudes, cognitive styles and emotional states of an individual are of crucial importance in determining whether a person will make an existential decision favoring suicide. The present study aims at precisely such an investigation; that is, a longitudinal examination of attitudes, cognitions and affects within a sample of suicidal threateners from the onset of the suicidal episode. Although most theoreticians have generally accepted the position that for the suicide life must be burdensome and painful and that death must have some attraction, this commonly held position has not been challenged or put to the test for at least two reasons: (1) because it is difficult to test; and (2) because of its compelling surface validity. There has been one exception to this trend, notably in the work of Neuringer (1960, 1961, 1967). It seems worthy at this point to review some of this incipient research and localize the scope of the present study within that research context.

PERTINENT BACKGROUND LITERATURE

Interest in the cognitive organization of suicidal thinking led Neuringer (1960, 1961, 1967, 1968, 1979a, 1979b) to study the cognitive and attitudinal aspects of thinking in suicidal individuals.

From the work of Shneidman (1957, 1969), in which the conception of dichotomous or polarized thinking was theoretically reformalized, Neuringer (1961) reported that hospitalized suicidal males who had made a wide variety of attempts, as well as another emotionally disturbed hospitalized group of males, tended to dichotomize their value systems as measured by the evaluative factor of the semantic differential more than normal hospitalized males. Neuringer (1967) found that a male suicidal-attempt group was unique in terms of dichotomizing the activity and strength of their thinking as measured by the activity and potency factors respectively of the semantic differential when compared to neurotic and normal male controls. In later studies Neuringer (1968, 1979a) reported that when level of suicidality was considered, excessive dichotomous thinking was found to be a pervasive aspect of seriously suicidal persons. Neuringer (1968) also reported that male suicidal attempters tended to organize their attitudes toward life and death in a more divergent manner than psychosomatic and normal hospitalized patients. It should be remarked that dichotomous thinking was measured by the degree of polarization or extremity of the semantic differential ratings for single concepts. Measures of divergent thinking were obtained by calculating the difference in semantic differential ratings between *two* concepts, such as life and death. Neuringer (1968) concluded that the suicidal persons perceived distinct differences between life and death. For them these existence alternatives are plainly juxtaposed, and this clear differentiation may be one of the conditions that makes a choice between life and death possible. The divergency in characterizations of life and death is certainly associated with suicidal persons' recent concerns with the value of living and dying. Neuringer felt that the divergent organization of attitudes toward life and death was related to the suicidal's tendency to think dichotomously, i.e., to polarize personally relevant events, objects, meanings and attitudes in such a manner as to experience them in their most extreme characterizations. Dichotomous thinking tendencies of this nature would polarize their feelings about death and life, making them strong alternative possibilities. The outcome of this thought process is of course lethal since compromises with life and death become difficult.

In related work, Neuringer (1964b) also reported that a suicidal-attempt group and another disturbed group (all males) were more labile in judging and reacting to interpersonal conflict situations than normal male subjects. This finding led the present investigators to speculate that the apparent polarization of attitudinal and cognitive processes, as evidenced by the prevalence of dichotomous and divergent thinking, and labile interpersonal judgments in suicidal persons, might also be characteristically prevalent in the affective and emotional states of these individuals. In the present investigation, this hunch was examined in terms of what Wessman and Ricks (1966) have called "affective complexity," but here is referred to as "affective polarization."

In a study of suicide notes, Spiegel and Neuringer (1963) found that the suicide notes left by males who completed suicide displayed more rigidity and inflexibility in thinking than the simulated (fake) notes written by a carefully matched group of control subjects. The nature of the effect of dread on suicidal behavior was also examined by Spiegel and Neuringer (1963) via comparison of genuine and simulated suicide notes. Thirty-three pairs of notes were used in the content analysis, and each pair of note-writers was carefully matched on a variety of epidemiological variables, including age, sex, race, marital status, socioeconomic status, religion and other factors. The authors concluded that lack of dread of death was a necessary but not sufficient condition for suicide to occur. The authors reported that: (1) genuine notes were judged to be less explicit in terms of intention to die than the simulated notes; (2) suicide or its synonyms were mentioned more often in the faked notes than in the genuine notes; (3) the genuine notes contained more instructions to the reader; and (4) judges rated the genuine notes as being more disorganized than the simulated notes. The study by Spiegel and Neuringer (1963) raised a question of particular relevance to the present investigation, namely the possibility of necessary shifts in cognitive and emotional states surrounding suicidal behavior. They proposed that suicide becomes possible when dread fails to arise because it has somehow been rendered unnecessary through self-deceptive maneuvers in which the individual believes he or she intends something other than suicide or avoids confronting the negative ramifications of a recognized suicidal intention.

In a related line of study, Neuringer (1970) measured the attitudes of an undifferentiated group of suicide attempters via a semantic differential questionnaire. Specifically, he obtained cross-sectional measurements within a two-week period following a suicidal attempt. He tentatively concluded that attitudes toward life tended to remain constant and slightly positive, while the attitudes toward death changed from neutral to negative valence. Later studies by Neuringer (1968, 1979b) indicate that severely suicidal males establish a negative attitude toward life as well as a positive characterization of life. Previous research (Neuringer, 1961) had used an omnibus group of suicidal individuals (i.e., patients at all levels of suicidal seriousness) and had not been able to identify differences between suicidal and nonsuicidal individuals in terms of differences in attitudes toward life and death.

PRESENT STUDY AS AN EXTENSION OF PREVIOUS WORK

The present study can be viewed as an extension of previous work in perhaps ten ways: (1) sex of subject sample; (2) study of threateners rather than attempters or committers; (3) utilization of a natural process rather than a retrospective analysis; (4) classification of subjects in terms of lethality levels of suicidality rather than omnibus suicide groups; (5) observation time extended from two to three weeks; (6) employment of longitudinal as opposed to cross-sectional observations; (7) examination of a variety of affective states; (8) investigation of affective complexity; (9) description of the interrelations among attitudinal, affective and cognitive characteristics of suicidal individuals; and (10) exploration of the relationship of subjects' self-reported suicidal potential to attitudinal and cognitive measures.

The majority of the cognitive and attitudinal literature on suicidal individuals (Neuringer, 1961, 1963, 1964a, 1964b,

1967, 1968, 1969a, 1969b) has focused on males. The present study has employed a female sample to counter-balance this trend.

Research literature has intensively examined suicide attempters and committers to the relative exclusion of suicide threateners. The sample employed here was comprised of individuals who were currently threatening suicide. Thus, if an individual called a suicide prevention agency and threaten-ed suicide he/she was classed as a threatener, regardless of the his or her past suicidal history. The selection procedure is more fully described in the next chapter. Of primary con-cern was the individual's present suicidal behavior. In this regard the present investigators' intention to observe suicidal behavior as it naturally occurred was germane. In this respect, a natural-process methodology (Shontz, 1965) was utilized rather than the prevalent retrospective analyses such as suicide-note analyses (Spiegel and Neuringer, 1963), psycho-logical autopsies and postattempt investigations (Neuringer, 1961, 1964b, 1967, 1968, 1979a, 1979b).

Because of the difficulty of obtaining a sufficiently large number of living suicidal persons, suicidologists have limited their research samples to either single cases or more often omnibus suicidal groups. Not until the advent of suicide prevention agencies was it feasible to design studies using larger and more selectively differentiated subject groups. The present investigation employed four subject groups (N = 40) which were differentiated on the basis of their suicidal potential levels. It was felt that such a design would be of aid in unraveling differences among various suicidal risk levels.

In light of the remarks of Neuringer (1970), it was decid-ed to extend the observation period to 3 weeks. While an even longer longitudinal span would have been desirable, feasibility of such a study diminished as a function of the increased investigative costs and potential subject sample attrition. It was thus decided that individuals in the present investigation were to be studied longitudinally for three weeks from the onset of a suicidal episode. It is useful at this point to discuss what is meant by "the onset of the suicidal episode" or "crisis." The onset of the episode was operationally defined as that point in time when the individual verbalized a suicide threat to a staff member of a suicide prevention agency. The term "suicidal episode" was employed to refer to the circumscribed period of 3 weeks following the verbalized communication of a suicidal threat. It was assumed that for an individual to threaten suicide that person was in a disruptive and generally stressful state — in short, a kind of crisis. For the present purposes, it was deemed unnecessary to further define or operationalize the terms "stress" or "crisis" other than to accept the individual's self-report that he was in a state of upset and stress.

In the following respects, the present study examined relatively unexplored suicidal phenomena: a variety of affective states were measured rather than just certain affects such as found in the work of Freud (1949) and Shneidman and Farberow (1957). Specifically, the present research utilized a principal components analysis to obtain measures of what Wessman and Ricks (1966) have called "affective complexity." Further P design factor analytic techniques were utilized to assess the interrelations among various attitudinal, cognitive and affective states, and thus aid in the formulation of a developmental model of stages or steps characteristic of individuals on the road to suicide. Finally, it was decided to explore the relationships of the suicidal persons self-reported suicidality to the obtained attitudinal and cognitive measures.

SIGNIFICANCE OF THE RESEARCH

The significance of the proposed research lies in the area of (1) its basic data-gathering procedure; and (2) providing clues to the status of suicidal persons.

The basic data-gathering procedure involved the repeated measurements of various attitudinal, cognitive and affective variables over a circumscribed period following the inception of the suicidal crisis. While the testing procedure is more fully described later it is worth mentioning that a mail-in procedure was effectively employed. Each person filled out the questionnaires on a daily basis and promptly mailed them back to the investigators. This technique freed the investigators from arranging daily testing appointments with each subject and consequently allowed the collection of data from a relatively larger sample of people. It had the further advantage of testing individuals relatively unobtrusively in their natural home settings. Furthermore, the research was significant in charting the course of the suicidal crisis from inception and might well supply the investigators with diagnostic and prognostic clues concerning the course of the suicidal thinking of persons who are self-destructive.

While there has been much speculation about the attitudes toward life and earth as well as the interrelationships among cognitive, attitudinal and affective variables in the suicidal individual, no empirical studies have been made. Generally, researcher's strategies involve the evaluation of the suicidal person, sifting through evidence to find out what kind of individual kills himself; discovering the signs or clues that could have predicted the behavior; determining the sociometric class most prone to suicidal behavior. This has led to a considerable degree of focusing on residuals (suicide notes, diaries, memories of friends, and relatives and other evidence). It was believed that the attitudes, cognitive styles and emotional states of an individual were of crucial importance in determining whether a person will make a suicidal choice. It was hoped that this study would provide basic data in this area and would also serve as a focal point for future research in suicide prevention.

SPECIFIC AIMS OF THE PRESENT RESEARCH

As has been cited above, the general aim of the investigation to be described below is the intensive study of cognitive, attitudinal and affective changes over time in suicidal individuals with specific reference to the study of (1) differences among various classes of suicidal individuals; and (2) comparative longitudinal changes within each of the groups. Specific investigative focus was concerned with (1) meanings and patterns of changes in meanings of certain important focal attitudes toward "life," "death," and "suicide"; (2) changes in certain cognitive organizations, in particular, dichotomous thinking, heretofore described as associated with suicidal thinking; and finally (3) affective states of various classes of suicidal individuals over a circumscribed time period.

To accomplish the goals of the research it was divided into three major phases or substudies. The investigative foci are here summarized.

In Study 1, both attitudinal and dichotomous thinking measures were examined with the intent of (1) differentiating the four subject groups in terms of their ratings for each of the attitudinal and cognitive items; and (2) detecting any clearly and simply patterned changes in these measures among groups following the onset of a suicidal episode. Of secondary interest was the examination of any correlation between (a) the attitudinal measures and the subject's self-reported suicidal lethality ratings; and (b) the dichotomous thinking measures and the self-reported suicidal lethality ratings.

The second study was primarily concerned with measurement of the affective states of suicidal persons. As in the first study, analyses were performed in order to (1) distinguish the four subject groups in terms of their affective indices; and (2) detect any simply and clearly patterned affective changes among the groups following the onset of a suicidal crisis.

Study 3 investigated the interrelationships among the attitudinal, cognitive and affective measures for certain representatively selected suicidal individuals. Of secondary interest was the exploration of whether the affective states of various suicidal individuals differed in degree of complexity or polarization.

CHAPTER

V

THE RESEARCH DESIGN

The goal of the present research was to gather information about the affective, attitudinal and cognitive states of various female suicidal threateners over time and to study the interrelations among these measures. To accomplish this goal the research was divided into three parts. One study dealt with suicidal women's attitudinal and cognitive measures; the second study investigated their affective indices and the third study carefully examined the relations between the affective measures and the cognitive and attitudinal features.

It should be clear that in all phases of the research the individuals were initially selected and treated identically; further, all of them were tested on all the affective, cognitive and attitudinal measures. It is important to note, however, that in Studies 1 and 2, all the data from all the subjects was analyzed while in the third phase of the study analysis focused upon data gathered from one representatively selected woman from each of the four types of suicidal groups. The distinction between the first two phases of the research and the last phase is one of differential sample size and statistical analysis rather than experimental treatment. In short, the sample size for each of the first two phases was $N = 40$, while the analyses employed in the third phase were performed four separate times on samples of $N = 1$.

In the third study, the intent was to carefully investigate the interrelationships among all the variables measured. In order to preserve the uniqueness of the interrelationships and also allow the intensive investigation of the data it was decided that a design employing representatively selected single cases would be statistically appropriate, theoretically heuristic and psychologically meaningful at this stage of suicidological research.

THE SUICIDAL WOMEN

The women in this study were obtained from the Los Angeles Suicide Prevention Center and the University of California at Los Angeles Medical Center.

The Los Angeles S.P.C. was established in 1958 for the evaluation, referral, treatment, follow-up and overall prevention of suicidal behavior. The center maintains a constant 24-hour telephone service serving the Los Angeles area. Persons treated by the center come from various sources: some are self-referrals; some are referrals by other agencies, friends, relatives, physicians and other professional persons. The U.C.L.A. Medical Center maintains extensive inpatient and outpatient treatment facilities for a variety of emotionally disturbed persons.

Four groups of women were tested: three suicidal threatener groups and one nonsuicidal comparison control group. The groups were defined in terms of lethality of suicidal intent on the basis of the Los Angeles Suicide Prevention Center's Assessment of Suicidal Potentiality Scale (Farberow, Heilig and Litman, 1968).

The Suicide Prevention Center Scale is a multidimensional instrument which weights differentially the following features of the suicidal person: (1) age and sex; (2) symptoms; (3) stress; (4) acute vs. chronic situation; (5) suicidal plan; (6) resources; (7) prior suicidal behavior; (8) medical status; (9) communication aspects; and (10) reaction of significant other.

Individuals who rated 0 on this scale were considered nonsuicidal and served as the comparison control group. Individuals who rated between 1–3 on the scale were characterized as having low lethal suicidal intentions. Ratings of 4–5 characterized moderate suicidal lethality intentions and ratings of 6–9 defined high suicidal intent. It should be noted that in the practical use of the scale, extreme ratings of 8 and 9 are usually reserved for suicide attempters; hence, the actually observed ratings range of 0–7 defined the present sample. The ratings were made by staff members of the Los Angeles Suicide Prevention Center.

For brevity, the suicidal groups will be referred to as the *LS* (low suicide intent), *MS* (moderate suicide intent), and *HS* (high suicide intent) groups. The nonsuicidal comparison group shall be termed the *C* (comparison) group.

Approach to Subjects

Daily reviews of new contacts to the S.P.C. and U.C.L.A. Medical Center were made and interviews were conducted with the first 40 subjects who met the general selection criteria of the research.

Each person was interviewed in order to (1) confirm the suicidal lethality rating; (2) explain the testing procedure; and (3) collect epidemiological and case history data. Consent for participation in the research was gained and the subjects were assured of the confidentiality of their reports.

General Selection Criteria

Three criteria were employed in selection: age, sex and suicidal potential. In all other respects, the samples were unselected and random.

Age. Participants were limited to the range of 18 to 60 years of age. Younger women were not used in order to avoid the special problems associated with youth and adolescence (Peck, 1968; Schrut, 1964). Older persons were not studied because of the possible effects that aging might have on cognitive organization.

Suicide potential: The suicidal women. The singularly important selection criterion was that the individual be "threatening suicide now." This criterion was assured in three ways: (1) the women called the Los Angeles Suicide Prevention Center (S.P.C.) and verbally threatened suicide; (2) the S.P.C. staff worker perceived the caller's communication as a suicide threat; and (3) at the time of the first interview-test session, the interviewer judged the individual's communication as suicide threats. Two further safeguards were utilized to insure that the "threatening suicide now" criterion was met: (a) if during the interval between the initial call to the S.P.C. and the first interview–test session the individual had made a suicide attempt, that individual was not considered an appropriate research participant; and (b) if the individual had made a suicide attempt within two weeks prior to the call to the S.P.C., that individual was also eliminated from the potential sample pool. These last two safeguards were employed as controls for the possibly confounding after-effects of a very recent suicidal attempt.

Suicide potential: The nonsuicidal women. For purposes of this research, it was decided that the comparison control women should be, as the suicidal participants were, in a state of current stress or crisis, with the important exception that they not be suicidal. In other words, one might label the comparison control groups as "in crisis, but not suicidal," and the suicidal groups as "in crisis and suicidal."

It was assumed that for an individual to threaten suicide that person was in a disruptive and generally stressful state — in short a state of crisis. For the nonsuicidal women, stressful states were characterized by financial hardships, marital disharmony, impending separations and divorces, interpersonal and family difficulties, recent loss of significant others and other factors. For the present purposes, it was deemed unnecessary to further define or operationalize the terms "stress" or "crisis" other than to accept the individual's self-report that she was in a state of upset and stress. It is useful at this point to reiterate what is meant by the onset of a suicidal episode or crisis. The onset of the crisis episode, be it suicidal or nonsuicidal, was operationally defined as that point in time when the individual verbalized her stressful condition to a staff member of the S.P.C. or the U.C.L.A. Medical Center. The terms "suicidal episode" and/or "crisis episode" were employed to refer to the circumscribed period of three weeks following the verbalized communication by that individual concerning her state of duress. For the suicidal women, the verbalized communication was a suicide threat; for the nonsuicidal person, the verbalized communication entailed statements concerning her general state of upset and stress.

In summary, when an individual was accepted as a potential participant, she was placed into one of the four groups, depending on her suicidal potential rating via the S.P.C. Assessment of Suicidal Potentiality Scale.

Specific Selection Criteria

The present research has been categorized into three interrelated substudies. The first study examined attitudinal and cognitive variables. The second study focused on affective variables; the third study investigated the interrelations among the attitudinal, cognitive and affective variables. In all studies the general selection criteria discussed above were maintained. The primary difference between Studies 1 and 2 vs. Study 3 was in the number of individuals whose data were analyzed.

Studies 1 and 2. In the first two studies everybody's data ($N = 40$) were analyzed. Other than the general selection criteria discussed above, there were no further selection criteria employed.

Study 3. In the third study dealing with the interrelationships among the affective, attitudinal and cognitive measure, the data from only one representative person from each of the four groups was analyzed ($N = 1$, replicated four times). What follows is a description of the selection procedure used in Study 3 for choosing one representative participant from each of the four subject groups.

Selection of representative subjects for Study 3

On the basis of epidemiological and case history data collected for each person, working tables were constructed for each group listing what seemed to be relevant and reliable epidemiological variables. From these tables one woman from each group was selected for intensive examination of the basis of her apparent "representativeness" within that group. Six epidemiological variables were examined: age, race, education, marital status, previous therapeutic contacts and previous suicide threats. A woman was considered representative of her group if she characterized an average or modal position on each of the six variables. In this study the representative nonsuicidal woman was 33 years of age, Caucasian, had 4 years of college, was married, had one previous therapeutic contact and had no history of suicide threats. The representative low-suicidal participant was 38 years old, Caucasian, had two years of college, was presently unmarried, had two or more previous therapeutic contacts, and had made two or more prior suicidal threats. The representative moderate-suicidal person was 41 years of age, Caucasian, had 2 years of college, was currently married, had two or more previous therapeutic contacts, and had made two or more prior suicidal threats. The representative high-suicidal individual was 38 years old, Caucasian, had a high school education, was presently unmarried, had two or more

prior therapeutic contacts, and had made two or more previous suicide threats.

THE ASSESSMENT PROCEDURE

In the first interview each participant was instructed how
to use the test booklets. Each subject was told that every day
for the next 21 days she was to fill out one attitude and cognition questionnaire and one affective state questionnaire.
Further, the participant was asked to mail back daily the previous day's completed questionnaires. This procedure assured
that the subject was actually completing the test materials
daily. The women were each given 21 daily face sheets, 21
attitudinal and cognitive questionnaires, 21 affective state
questionnaires and 21 postage-paid return-mail envelopes.
Because they had to fill out the questionnaire on a daily
basis, their motivational level was maintained by daily pay-
ments of $2.00 for each set of data; they were not paid until
all questionnaires had been completed. It should be clear that
each person filled out the same materials daily and mailed
them each day to the investigators.

The Test Booklets

Each individual filled out two test booklets on a daily
basis for 21 days. In addition, they responded to a daily
face sheet which gathered general information.

In light of some preliminary findings (Neuringer, 1966)
based on an observation period of two weeks it was decided
to extend the observation time to cover a three-week span.
Neuringer's (1966) data suggested the possibility that some
regularly patterned attitudinal changes might exist in suicidal
persons following a suicidal incident.

Face sheet. The face sheet was used to gather general
information, daily suicidal status, behavioral activities,
medical and health data and daily self-lethality reports.

Attitudinal and cognitive questionnaire. The Semantic Differential method developed by Osgood, Suci and Tannenbaum (1957) was utilized for (1) measurement of attitudes toward various concepts of interest and (2) measurement of the cognitive process of extreme or dichotomous thinking. The Semantic Differential method was developed to objectively measure the meaning of various concepts and consists of various bipolar scales representing three meaning factors: Evaluation, Activity and Potency. It is possible to derive the position of a concept along these three factors from the bipolar judgments made to the concept by a subject. The form used consisted of nine concepts (life, death, suicide, murder, myself, other people, my past, my life now, my future). The order of presentation of the concepts was randomized for each test booklet. Only those scales high on the Evaluation, Activity and Potency factors were employed. In this study, nine evaluative scales (good − bad, dirty − clean, nice − awful, unpleasant − pleasant, fair − unfair, worthless − valuable, happy − sad, dishonest − honest and beautiful − ugly) were used. The Activity scales were passive − active, fast − slow, cold − hot and sharp − dull. The Potency scales that were employed were strong − weak, small − large, hard − soft, light − heavy and rugged − delicate.

Affective state questionnaire

The Personal Feeling Scale developed by Wessman and Ricks (1966) was used to assess emotional state. This scale is a multivariate instrument which yields information along 16 categories of mood: fullness vs. emptiness of life; receptivity toward and stimulation by the world; social respect vs. social contempt; personal freedom vs. external constraint; harmony vs. anger; own sociability vs. withdrawal; companionship vs. being isolated; love and sex; present work; thought processes; tranquillity vs. anxiety; impulse expression vs. self-restraint; personal moral judgment; self-confidence vs. feeling of inadequacy; energy vs. fatigue; elation vs. depression.

Scoring the Test Booklets

Attitudinal measures. Each concept was measured on each of the three semantic differential factors contained in the Attitudinal and Cognitive Questionnaire: evaluation, activity and potency. The range of scores for each concept on each factor was 1–7. A low score on the evaluation factor indicated the subject valued the concept; similarly low scores on the activity and potency factors indicated that the concept was rated as active and potent respectively. High scores on the factors indicated that the concept was devalued (negatively evaluated) and perceived as passive and as impotent respectively. For example, if a concept received the low score of 1 on the evaluation factor, it suggested that the subject regarded the concept as generally good, clean, nice, pleasant, fair, valuable, happy, honest and beautiful. A high score of 7 indicated the concept was rated as generally bad, dirty, awful, unpleasant, unfair, worthless, sad, dishonest and ugly.

Cognitive measures. A measure of the extremity of rating – here called dichotomous thinking – was obtained by a simple arithmetic transformation of the initial semantic differential attitude scores. The resultant score is called a D score. The arithmetic procedure can alternatively be viewed as (1) a procedure in which the most extreme scores are weighted more heavily than the less extreme scores or (2) as a subtraction procedure in which initial attitude scores are subtracted from the absolute value of 4. In other words, D score $= / 4 / - /$ attitude score $/$.

A D score of 0 was interpreted to mean an absence of extreme or dichotomous thinking, while a D score of 3 suggested maximal dichotomous thinking.

Affective measures. There were 16 aspects of mood which were measured by the affective state questionnaire. The range of scores for each mood aspect was 1 to 10. High scores (e.g., a score of 10 indicated that the person felt fullness of life, receptivity toward the world, social respect, freedom, harmony, sociability, companionship, confidence, energy and general elation. Low scores indicated the opposite feelings — in short, a general feeling of emptiness and depression. For each of the 16 mood scales each person was asked to indicate which one of the 10 scale points best depicted her lowest feeling, her highest feeling and the point that best characterized her average feeling for the day. For purposes of this research only the average ratings for each scale were analyzed.

RESEARCH DESIGNS AND ANALYSES

Study 1: Attitudinal and Cognitive Measures

The general experimental design employed was a 21 X 4 repeated measurements design. The two independent variables were suicidal groups (4) and days from suicidal incident (21). Only three concepts of primary interest were analyzed (life, death, suicide) on each of the three semantic factors (evaluation, activity, potency) for each of the two types of measure (attitudinal scores, D scores). In total, 18 analyses of variance were performed.

This design yielded information about the longitudinal change on the attitudinal and cognitive measures among the groups.

A second analysis examined the correlations between the suicidal group's daily self-lethality ratings and the attitudinal and cognitive measures. Specifically for each of the three suicidal groups (*LS* group, *MS* group and *HS* group) a correlation coefficient was calculated between a group's daily self-lethality ratings and each of the three concepts (life, death, suicide) on each of the three semantic factors (evaluation, activity, potency) for each of the two measures (attitudinal scores, D scores). Thus for each group 18 correlation coefficients were computed, giving a grand total of 54 correlation coefficients for all three groups. It should be noted that for the *C* group, daily self-lethality ratings were consistently scored as absent, and hence displayed no variance over days or between subjects. In light of this fact, correlational analyses for the C group were considered statistically inappropriate and for the present purposes, psychologically irrelevant; consequently, these correlations were not included in the final analyses. The primary purpose of the correlational analyses was to examine whether the suicidal subjects' self-ratings of daily suicidal potential reflected any relationship to the attitudinal and cognitive ratings.

Study 2: Affective Measures

The basic experimental design utilized was a 21 X 4 repeated measurements analysis of variance. The two independent variables were suicidal groups (4), and days from suicidal incident (21). Each of the 16 scales on Wessman and Ricks (1966) Personal Feeling Scale were separately analyzed. Thus a total of 16 analyses of variance (mixed model) were calculated. This design supplied information about the longitudinal change on the affective measures among the subject groups.

Study 3: Interrelationship among Affective, Attitudinal and Cognitive Measures

In order to evaluate the interrelationships among the attitudinal, cognitive and affective measures, each of the four representative subject's data were analyzed by the P design factor analytic method (Cattell, 1946; Cattell, Cattell and Rhymer, 1947). The P design is based on repeated measures from a single subject. Intercorrelations are determined among measures and the final factors reflect the stability of relations between the measures over time. Specifically, the method of principal axes or principal components was employed for each initial factor analysis (Harmon, 1960); then the factors were rotated, using Kaiser's (1958) varimax criterion rotation. A discussion of the merit of principal components analysis can be found in Nunnally (1967).

In summary, four separate P design factor analyses were performed, one analysis for each subject.

A second analysis using P design explored each of the four representative subject's affective data. The analysis was stopped after principal components were derived. Wessman and Ricks (1966) suggest that "the number of factors produced by a person is a relatively precise indication of the extent to which the feelings that he records all vary together, as an all-or-none phenomenon, or move in a relatively differentiated and independent fashion. If the number of measuring scales is held constant, as it was here in each group, this number can therefore be considered an index of affective complexity (p. 73)."

VI

STUDY 1:
THINKING (ATTITUDES AND COGNITION)*

The results presented in this chapter have been divided into five parts: (1) analyses of attitudinal measures; (2) analysis of divergent thinking (life vs. death); (3) analyses of dichotomous thinking measures; (4) correlational analyses of daily self-rated suicidal lethality with attitudinal data; and (5) correlational analyses of daily self-rated suicidal lethality with dichotomous thinking data.

PART 1: ANALYSES OF ATTITUDINAL
MEASURES

Each of the 9 attitudinal measures were examined independently by means of analyses of variance. The appropriateness of each analysis was first verified by computation of

* A list of the tables referred to in this chapter may be found in Appendix A.

Bartlett's test for homogeneity of variance. When statistically significant findings were indicated, Duncan's multiple range test was employed.

Each analysis of variance examined whether an attitudinal measure yielded significant differences between groups, days and groups X days interactions.

Summary of Findings

Three attitudinal measures yielded significant differences among the 4 groups. None of the attitudinal measures were significant for the variable of days or for the groups X days interaction terms.

For each of the 3 semantic differential factors — evaluation, activity and potency — the score range was 1 to 7. A low score of 1 indicated that the concept was rated as highly valued, active and potent, while a high score of 7 indicated that the concept was devalued, perceived as inactive and weak on each of the respective factors.

Significant attitudinal measures differences were found for (a) the evaluation of life (b) the activity of death and (c) the activity of suicide. In particular, the *LS* and *C* groups evaluated life significantly more positively than the *HS* group; the *LS* group rated death significantly less active than the *HS* group; furthermore, the *LS* group rated suicide significantly less active than each of the other groups. These conclusions were drawn from Table 1 — Summary of analyses of variance on attitudinal measures, and Table 2 — Summary of Duncan's multiple range tests on attitudinal measures. The rest of this section examines the findings in closer detail.

Detailed Findings

The following subsections of Part 1 review and interpret each attitudinal measure in terms of the following tables: (1) table of groups X days means and standard deviations;

and (2) analysis of variance source table. It was not the researchers' intent to examine the similarities and differences among various attitudinal measures within a single subject group, but to investigate the similarities and differences among the groups for each attitudinal measure separately.

Life: Evaluation. The groups differed significantly in their attitudinal ratings. Specifically the *HS* group rated life less valuable than did the *LS* and *C* groups. These conclusions are drawn from Table 3 — Means and standard deviations for attitudinal evaluations of life; and Table 4 — Analysis of variance for attitudinal evaluations of life.

Life: Activity. None of the variables tested by an analysis of variance were significant. The observations are based on Table 5 — Means and standard deviations of attitudinal activity of life, and Table 6 — Analysis of variance of attitudinal activity of life.

Life: Potency. No significant findings were revealed by an analysis of variance. These conclusions are based on Table 7 — Means and standard deviations of attitudinal potency of life, and Table 8 — Analysis of variance for attitudinal potency of life.

Death: Evaluation. No variables tested by the analysis of variance reached significant levels. These observations are based on Table 9 — Means and standard deviations for attitudinal evaluations of death, and Table 10 — Analysis of variance for evaluative attitudes of death.

Death: Activity. The groups differed significantly in their ratings. In fact, the *HS* group rated death as significantly more active than did the *LS* group. These interpretations are based on Table 11 — Means and standard deviations for attitudinal activity of death, and Table 12 — Analysis of variance for attitudinal activity of death.

Death: Potency. No significant findings were revealed by an analysis of variance. These conclusions come from an interpretation of Table 13 — Means and standard deviations for attitudinal potency of death, and Table 14 — Analysis of variance for attitudinal potency of death.

Suicide: Evaluation. None of the variables investigated by an analysis of variance reached significance. These inferences were drawn from Table 15 — Means and standard deviations for attitudinal evaluations of suicide, and Table 16 — Analysis of variance for attitudinal evaluation of suicide.

Suicide: Activity. An analysis of variance revealed significant group differences. In particular, the *LS* group rated suicide significantly less active than did any of the other three groups. These interpretations are based on an examination of Table 17 — Means and standard deviations for attitudinal activity of suicide, and Table 18 — Analysis of variance for attitudinal activity of suicide.

Suicide: Potency. No significant findings were revealed. These conclusions are based on a perusal of Table 19 — Means and standard deviations for attitudinal potency of suicide, and Table 20 — Analysis of variance for attitudinal potency of suicide.

PART 2: ANALYSIS OF DIVERGENT
THINKING (LIFE VS. DEATH)

The argument that attitudinal divergency between life and death may be a crucial component of serious suicidal thinking was statistically examined in terms of divergency scores. A divergency score was computed by calculating the absolute difference between ratings for the concepts life and death. Each of three semantic differential factors (evaluation, activity, potency) was tested separately by one-way analyses of variance. The one-way analyses examined whether the four groups differed in terms of attitudinal divergency measures. Two of the three attitudinal factors (viz., evaluation and activity) significantly differentiated the groups in terms of divergency scores. The preceding findings are based on an analysis of Table 21 — Summary of Duncan's multiple range tests on divergent thinking measures.

Divergent Evaluative Attitudes

The following observations were drawn from Table 22 — Analysis of variance on attitudinal divergency for the evaluative factor. The *HS* and *C* groups, while significantly different from each other, were also significantly different from all other groups in terms of life vs. death divergent thinking. It should be recalled that divergency measures are computed from the absolute difference between the ratings for life and death. The finding that both the *C* and *HS* group think divergently is better understood in light of the previous findings which revealed that the *HS* group rated life as significantly less positive than did the *C* group. *Thus an interesting reversal was discovered: While both the C and HS groups view life vs. death as divergent, the C group evaluates life positively and death negatively in contrast to the HS group which devalues life and positively values death. It is precisely this reversal of the valences for life and death which apparently earmarks serious suicidality.*

Divergent Activity Attitudes

The following observations are based on an inspection of Table 23 — Analysis of variance on attitudinal divergency for the activity factor. Analyses indicated that the *HS* group is significantly less divergent than all other groups in the attitudinal ratings of the activities of life vs. death, while the *LS* group displays significantly more divergency than all other groups. Related findings indicated all groups tended to rate the activity of life as generally neutral with no significant group differences; *however, the* HS *group rated death as significantly more active than the* LS *group.* It would seem that while both the *HS* and *LS* group display divergent thinking in terms of the activity of life vs. death, the *LS* group is essentially different from the *HS* group in terms of the position on the activity–passivity continuum for the attitude of death. The *LS* group views death as passive; the *HS* group views it as active. It is plausible to suggest that a passive view of death (as in the *LS* group) may be an effective coping technique whereby death ideation can commence and flourish in a relatively non-dread-inducing manner. Furthermore, it seems quite possible that once death ideation is manifested and coped with at a minimal level, it can then become a dominant theme in the thoughts of the potentially self-destructive person. Findings from Study 3 revealed a progression of death ideation in suicidal individuals that begins with a general death concern in the low suicidal level, advances to death myopia in the moderately suicidal state and culminates in the conceptualization of death as a way to freedom in the seriously suicidal stage. *In short, at the most lethal stage of suicidality, death is viewed as a liberator and by implication the suicidal alternative is enhanced.*

Divergent Potency Attitudes

The one-way analysis of variance for the potency aspects of life vs. death divergent thinking did not reach significant levels. This conclusion was drawn from Table 24 — Analysis of variance on attitudinal divergency for the potency factor.

PART 3: ANALYSES OF DICHOTOMOUS THINKING MEASURES

The nine dichotomous thinking measures were separately analyzed by analyses of variance. A Bartlett's test for homogeneity of variance within groups was first calculated to check the appropriateness of each analysis of variance. Duncan's multiple range test was employed to further examine any statistically significant findings revealed by the analysis of variance.

Each analysis of variance investigated whether a dichotomous thinking measure yielded significant differences between groups, days and groups X days interactions.

Summary of Findings

Three dichotomous thinking measures evidenced significant differences between groups ($p < .05$). None of the dichotomous thinking measures was significant for the variable of days or for the groups X days interactions.

For each of the three semantic differential factors (viz., evaluation, activity, potency) the score range was 0 to 3. Low scores near 0 indicated that the cognitive process of dichotomous thinking was absent or minimally present, while higher scores approaching 3 evidenced much or maximal dichotomous thinking.

The significant cognitive measures were for the evaluation of life and the strength or potency of life and suicide. It is worth mention that the activity of life and the potency of death very closely approached significance at the .05 level. The critical ratio for significance ($p < .05$) was 2.861. For the purposes of discussion, however, only those measures which clearly reached significance have been discussed. These conclusions were based on Table 25 – Summary of analyses of variance on dichotomous thinking measures.

The following remarks are based on Table 26 – Summary of Duncan's multiple range tests on dichotomous thinking measures. Orthogonal comparisons performed on the significant findings revealed that (1) the *HS* group evaluated life significantly more dichotomously than did the *MS* and *C* groups; (2) the *HS* group rated the potency of life significantly more dichotomously than did the *MS* and *C* groups; and (3) the *HS* group scored the potency of suicide significantly more dichotomously than did the *MS* group. In general, the *HS* group rated the concepts most dichotomously; and in particular for the evaluation and potency of life, the *HS* and *LS* groups tended to rate more dichotomously than did the *MS* and *C* groups. This tendency for the *HS* and *LS* groups is supported by some of the factor analytic findings of Study 3 in which the *HS* and *LS* subjects clearly displayed a dichotomous thinking factor. The rest of this section examines the findings in closer detail.

Detailed Findings

The next 9 subsections of Part 3 present and examine each dichotomous thinking measure in terms of the following tables: (1) table of groups X days means and standard deviations; and (2) analysis of variance source table. It should be restated that for the present purposes, it was the researchers' primary intent to examine the similarities and differences among the groups for each dichotomous thinking measure separately.

Life: Evaluation. The groups differed significantly in their dichotomous ratings. Specifically the *HS* group rated life more dichotomously than did the *MS* and *C* groups. These observations are based on an inspection of Table 27 — Means and standard deviations for dichotomous evaluations of life, and Table 28 — Analysis of variance for dichotomous evaluations of life.

Life: Activity. None of the variables tested by an analysis of variance were significant. This conclusion is based on Table 29 — Means and standard deviations for dichotomous activity of life, and Table 30 — Analysis of variance for dichotomous activity of life.

Life: Potency. An analysis of variance indicated that the groups differed significantly in their ratings. In fact, the *HS* group rated the potency of life significantly more dichotomously than did the *MS* and *C* groups. This inference is based on Table 31 — Means and standard deviations for dichotomous potency of life, and Table 32 — Analysis of variance for dichotomous potency of life.

Death: Evaluation. No variables tested by the analysis of variance reached significant levels. This conclusion is based on Table 33 — Means and standard deviations for dichotomous evaluations of death, and Table 34 — Analysis of variance for dichotomous evaluations of death.

Death: Activity. No variables tested by an analysis of variance were significant. This observation is based on Table 35 — Means and standard deviations for dichotomous activity of death, and Table 36 — Analysis of variance for dichotomous activity of death.

Death: Potency. While none of the variables reached significance at $p = .05$, the group variable on this cognitive measure closely approached significance. The preceding comment is based on an inspection of Table 37 — Means and standard deviations for dichotomous potency of death, and Table 38 — Analysis of variance for dichotomous potency of death.

Suicide: Evaluation. The analysis of variance source table revealed no significant variables. This conclusion is based on Table 39 — Means and standard deviations for dichotomous evaluations of suicide, and Table 40 — Analysis of variance for dichotomous evaluations of suicide.

Suicide: Activity. None of the variables tested by an analysis of variance were significant. This observation is drawn from an inspection of Table 41 — Means and standard deviations for dichotomous activity of suicide, and Table 42 — Analysis of variance for dichotomous activity of suicide.

Suicide: Potency. The following remarks are based on Table 43 — Means and standard deviations for dichotomous potency of suicide, and Table 44 — Analysis of variance for dichotomous potency of suicide. An analysis of variance revealed significant group differences. In particular, the *HS* group rated the concept significantly more dichotomously than did the *MS* group.

PART 4: CORRELATION ANALYSES OF DAILY SELF-RATED SUICIDAL LETHALITY WITH ATTITUDINAL DATA

The following conclusions are based on Table 45 — Table of correlations for self-rated lethality with attitudinal data. Each subject was asked on a daily basis to rate her suicidal potential via the Face Sheet described in Chapter V. A product-moment correlation coefficient ("r") was calculated on the daily suicidal ratings with each of the 9 attitudinal measures. This was done for each of the 3 groups of suicidal subjects (*LS, MS, HS,* groups). The correlation analyses were not performed on the *C* group data because such analyses seemed statistically inappropriate and psychologically irrelevant. In total, 27 (3 X 9) coefficients were computed so as to examine the possible associations between self-reported suicidal ratings with the attitudinal data.

The evaluation factor for all three concepts (life, death, suicide) was significantly correlated with the self-ratings for all the groups. Findings indicated that for the concept of life, increases in self-rated suicidal lethality were significantly associated with increases in the negative evaluation of life. Alternatively, as the individual felt less suicidal, she rated life more positively. For the concepts death and suicide (evaluative factor) increases in self-rated suicidality were significantly associated with decreases in the positive evaluation of these concepts. In other words, as self-rated suicidality decreased, death and suicide were rated more negatively on the evaluative factor.

PART 5: CORRELATION ANALYSES OF DAILY SELF-RATED SUICIDAL LETHALITY WITH DICHOTOMOUS THINKING DATA

The following comments are based on a perusal of Table 46 — Table of correlations for self-rated lethality with dichotomous thinking data. Product-moment correlation coefficients ("r") were calculated on the daily suicidal potential ratings and each of the 9 dichotomous thinking measures for each of the 3 suicidal groups. Thus a total of 27 (3 X 9) coefficients were computed. The purpose of these analyses was to afford an examination of the association between self-rated suicidal potential and dichotomous thinking.

For the *HS* group, the concepts life and death (evaluative factor) were rated more dichotomously as self-reported suicidality increased. There was also a slight tendency for the *HS* group to rate life's potency more dichotomously as suicidality increased. The findings suggested that dichotomous thinking may have been an influential and characteristic aspect of the cognitive processes in high-suicidal subjects so as to display a significant association with the subject's verbalized assessment of her own suicidal potential.

VII

STUDY 2: FEELINGS*

The data presented in this chapter focus on the affective information collected from all groups over the three week testing period. Sixteen different measures of affective or mood states were separately examined by analyses of variance. The appropriateness of each variance analysis was first checked by calculation of Bartlett's test for homogeneity of variance within groups. When statistically significant findings were indicated in the analyses of variance, Duncan's multiple range test was utilized. Each analysis of variance examined whether an affective measure yielded significant differences between groups, days and groups X days interactions.

* A list of the tables referred to in this chapter may be found in Appendix A.

SUMMARY OF FINDINGS

Nine of the 16 affective indices yielded significant differences among the 4 subject groups. None of the affective measures were significant for the variable of days, nor for the groups X days interaction terms.

For each of the 16 affective state measures, the scale range was 1 to 10. Low scores (e.g., 1) anchored the negative ends of the affective scales, while high scores (e.g., 10) anchored the positive ends of the scales. The Wessman and Ricks (1966) Personal Feeling Scale has been described in Chapter V.

The following mood states indicated significant group differences: fullness vs. emptiness of life; receptivity toward and stimulation by the world; harmony vs. anger; satisfaction with present work; readiness and value of thought processes; tranquillity vs. anxiety; personal moral judgment; self-confidence vs. feeling of inadequacy; and elation vs. depression.

The following observations are based on an analysis of Table 47 — Summary of findings by analyses of variance for affective data, and Table 48 — Summary of Duncan's multiple range tests on affective data. The general finding was that the C women's affective measures were characteristically more positively valenced than any of the other participant's measures; in particular the C women rated their affective states as significantly more positive than did the HS females. Stated alternately, the affective ratings of the HS women tended to be localized around the more negative ends of the affective scales; the ratings for the LS and MS groups were focalized in the middle-scale ranges; and the C women's ratings were more positively oriented. An examination of the patterns of significant group differences (Table 48) suggested that (1) the C and MS women were affectively similar (in no instances were there significant differences between the C and MS groups; and (2) the LS and MS females appeared affectively similar (in no cases were there significant group differences). (3) The highly negative affect of the *HS* women is singular (i.e., clearly different from all the other participants).

It should be cautioned that average group measures on affective states may be obfuscated by wide individual and daily affective variability. This is supported by the relatively large standard deviations for each group's affective indices. It is here recommended that this problem be handled in future research by intensive examination of each individual's affective data with particular regard to the degree of mood fluctuations. It is further recommended that measures be obtained on each individual's highest, lowest and average daily mood states. A potentially interesting measure of daily fluctuation may be obtained when the difference between the highest and lowest daily mood ratings for one dimension of mood at a time is calculated.

It has been tentatively suggested that the moderately suicidal women should display less daily mood variability than the other participants. The moderately suicidal individual is in an ambivalent and relatively valenceless state in which she may be trapped in the middle or neutral region of the life vs. death decision. Although the findings from Studies 1 and 3 lend support to this notion, the results from Study 2 in their present form can not be employed either to confirm or negate this contention. The rest of the chapter reports the findings in detail.

DETAILED FINDINGS

The next 16 subsections present and examine each affective measure in terms of the following tables: (1) table of groups X days means and standard deviations; and (2) analysis of variance source table.

1. *Fullness vs. emptiness of life (how emotionally satisfying, abundant or empty your life felt today).* An analysis of variance indicated significant group differences but no significant differences for the variable of days or for the groups X days interactions. Specifically, the *HS* group rated

life significantly more empty than did the *MS* and *C* groups. This conclusion is based on Table 49 — Means and standard deviation for fullness vs. emptiness of life, and Table 50 — Analysis of variance on fullness vs. emptiness of life.

2. *Receptivity toward and stimulation by the world (how interested and responsive you felt to what was going on around you).* An analysis of variance indicated that only the variable of groups reached significance. In particular, the *HS* group felt significantly less receptive to the world than did the *C* group. This finding is in accord with the results of Study 3 in which it is argued that high levels of suicidal potential are characterized by increased isolation from and decreased receptivity toward the social context. These observations are based on Tables 51 and 52 dealing with the means, standard deviations and the analysis of variance for receptivity toward the world.

3. *Social respect vs. social contempt (how you felt other people regarded you or felt about you today).* None of the variables tested reached significant levels. This conclusion is drawn from Table 53 — Means and standard deviations for social respect vs. social contempt, and Table 54 — Analysis of variance on social respect vs. social contempt.

4. *Personal freedom vs. external constraint (how much you felt you were free or not free to do as you wanted).* An analysis of variance indicated the absence of any significant variables. This observation is based on Tables 55 and 56 dealing with the means, standard deviations and analysis of variance for personal freedom vs. external constraint.

5. *Harmony vs. anger (how well you got along with, or how angry you felt toward other people).* The analysis of variance indicated significant group differences, but no significant differences for the variable of days or for the groups X days interactions. Specifically the *HS* group felt significantly more angry and less harmonious toward other people than did the *C* group. These observations are based on Table 57 — Means and standard deviations for harmony vs. anger, and Table 58 — Analysis of variance for harmony vs. anger.

6. *Own sociability vs. withdrawal (how socially outgoing or withdrawn you felt today).* An analysis of variance reported no significant differences among the groups, days, or groups X days interactions. The preceding conclusion is based on Table 59 — Means and standard deviations for own sociability vs. withdrawal, and Table 60 — Analysis of variance for own sociability vs. withdrawal.

7. *Companionship vs. being isolated (the extent to which you felt emotionally accepted by or isolated from other people).* An analysis of variance indicated that none of the variables tested reached significant levels. The previous conclusion is based on an inspection of Tables 61 and 62 dealing with the means, standard deviations and analysis of variance for companionship vs. being isolated.

8. *Love and sex (the extent to which you felt loving and tender or sexually frustrated and unloving).* The variance analysis showed that none of the variables of interest were significant. This conclusion is based on Tables 63 and 64 dealing with the means, standard deviations and analysis of variance for love and sex.

9. *Present work (how satisfied or dissatisfied you were with your work).* An analysis of variance indicated that the *HS* women were significantly more dissatisfied with work than the *C, LS* and *MS* groups. This finding is in accord with the findings that the *HS* group is least receptive and stimulated by the world, and also that the *HS* group find life rather empty. These inferences are based on an inspection of Table 65 -- Means and standard deviations for present work, and Table 66 — Analysis of variance for present work.

10. *Thought processes (how readily your ideas came and how valuable they seemed).* The following remarks are based on Table 67 — Means and standard deviations for thought processes, and Table 68 — Analysis of variance for thought processes. An analysis of variance found significant group differences. In particular the *HS* and *LS* groups reported their ideas to be significantly less accessible or valuable than did the *C* group. This result lends support to some of the other findings which indicated that the *HS* and *LS* groups

may be similar in experiencing the effects of a suicide-related depressive state.

11. *Tranquillity vs. anxiety (how calm or troubled you felt)*. The variance analysis indicated that the C and MS groups were significantly more tranquil and less troubled than the HS group; furthermore the LS group was significantly more anxious and less tranquil than the C group. This finding suggests, among other things, that the MS and C groups are affectively similar in terms of tranquillity vs. anxiety; and moreover there is the tendency for the HS and LS groups to be alike in that they are less tranquil than either the C or MS groups. This tendency gains support from the factor analytic findings of Study 3 (presented in the next chapter) in which it is contended that the C and MS groups are less depressed than either the LS or HS groups. The preceding observations are based on an inspection of Table 69 – Means and standard deviations for tranquillity vs. anxiety, and Table 70 – Analysis of variance for tranquillity vs. anxiety.

12. *Impulse expression vs. self-restraint (how expressive and impulsive or internally restrained and controlled you felt)*. An analysis of variance indicated that none of the variables tested reached significant levels. This conclusion is drawn from Tables 71 and 72 dealing with the means, standard deviations and the analysis of variance for impulse expression vs. self-restraint.

13. *Personal moral judgment (how self-approving or how guilty you felt)*. An analysis of variance indicated that the HS female reported significant less self-approval and more guilt than did the C, LS and MS groups. For the HS group, the mean scale item read as follows: "I have a sense of having done wrong." This conclusion is based on Table 73 – Means and standard deviations for personal moral judgment, and Table 74 – Analysis of variance for personal moral judgment.

14. *Self-confidence vs. feeling of inadequacy (how self-assured and adequate or helpless and inadequate you felt)*. The following observations are based on Table 75 – Means and standard deviations for self-confidence vs. feelings of

inadequacy, and Table 76 — Analysis of variance for self-confidence vs. feelings of inadequacy. An analysis of variance indicated that the *HS* group rated themselves significantly less self-confident than did the *MS* and *C* groups; furthermore, the *C* group reported significantly more self-confidence than either the *LS* or *HS* groups. This finding gains support from the results of Study 3 in which a self-confidence factor appeared only for the control subject.

15. *Energy vs. fatigue (how energetic or tired and weary you felt).* The analysis of variance indicated that none of the variables tested reached significant levels. This conclusion is based on Tables 77 and 78 dealing with the means, standard deviations and analysis of variance for energy vs. fatigue.

16. *Elation vs. depression (how elated or depressed, happy or unhappy you felt today).* An analysis of variance indicated that the *HS* women were significantly more unhappy and depressed than either the *MS, LS,* or *C* groups. The preceding conclusion was drawn from Table 79 — Means and standard deviations for elation vs. depression, and Table 80 — Analysis of variance for elation vs. depression.

VIII

STUDY 3:
THINKING AND FEELING RELATIONSHIPS*

The results of Study 3 consists of two parts. Part 1 contains a principal components analysis of the affective data for each of the four representative females. Part 2 presents four factor analyses (rotated) — one analysis for each representative participant. Each factor analysis was based on all the combined data (i.e., affective, attitudinal and cognitive) available for each representative subject. The comments made in this chapter are based on a study of Table 81 — Summary of principle components analyses on affective state data, Table 82 — Summary of the affective scale means for the representatational subjects, Table 83 — Summary of rotated factor analytic findings, Tables 84 to 87 dealing with the affective-cognitive correlation matrices for the representational subjects, and Tables 88 to 91 dealing with the affective-cognitive factor rotations for each representational subject.

* A list of the tables referred to in this chapter may be found in Appendix A.

PART 1: PRINCIPAL COMPONENTS ANALYSES
OF AFFECTIVE DATA

For each of the four representative women, a principal components analysis (P design) was computed on her affective data. The intent of such a procedure was to examine the minimum number of principal (unrotated) factors necessary to account for the bulk of the variance. Following the suggestions of Wessman and Ricks (1966), such an analysis might reveal differences in affective complexity among the various suicidal lethality levels. It was felt that one of the characteristics of increased suicidal potential would be concomitant with decreased affective complexity in much the same way that increased suicidal lethality was associated with decreased cognitive complexity (i.e., increased dichotomous thinking).

Summary of Principal Components Analyses

The findings of the principal components analyses indicate that the C woman required 5 principal unrotated factors to account for the bulk of her affective data variance; the LS female required 3 factors, the MS needed only 1 factor; and the HS subject's affective variance was accounted for by 2 factors — 1 large factor, and 1 relatively small factor. The findings tended to support the speculation that high levels of suicidality are associated with decreased affective complexity. It should be further noted that while the results suggested a strong inverse correlation between suicidality and affective complexity, the association was not perfectly linear. In fact the MS female, rather than the HS female, displayed the least amount of complexity. This finding fits well with the arguments discussed elsewhere that (1) the HS woman, once she has taken some stand on the life vs. death issue, now has some free affect available; and (2) the MS female has all her affective energies invested in deciding on an existential stance.

PART 2: FACTOR ANALYSES ON THE AFFECTIVE, ATTITUDINAL AND COGNITIVE DATA

For each representative subject, a P design factor analysis was computed on the subject's combined attitudinal, affective and cognitive measures. To aid an examination of the correlation matrices and factor loading tables, a numerically keyed listing of the variables utilized in the analyses is presented in Appendix B. The "v" numbers described below represent the numbered variables or items, listed in Appendix B, which contributed to each of the following factors.

Factors Found for Representative Nonsuicidal Participant

Factor 1: General affecto-cognitive state. This factor is described by the following variables: general elation (v.'s 1, 2, 3, 4, 5, 7, 8, 11, 16), evaluation of life (v. 17); life is rated less dichotomously (v.'s: 26, 28). Explained variance: 19%.

Factor 2: Involvement with environment. This factor is described by the following variables: receptivity toward the world (v. 2), social respect (v. 3), personal freedom (v. 4), sociability (v. 6), companionship (v. 7), satisfaction with work (v. 9), active thought processes (v. 10), self-confidence (v. 14), and energy (v. 15). Explained variance: 20%.

Factor 3: Life energy factor: This factor is described by the following variables: energy (v. 15), life as active (v. 18). Explained variance: 9%.

Factor 4: Outer-directed anger. This factor is described by the following variables: anger (v. 5), devaluation of death (v. 20), death is rated dichotomously (v. 29). Explained variance: 10%.

Factor 6: Self-confidence. This factor is described by the following variables: self-confidence (v. 14), life as active (v. 19), death as passive (v. 21), and impotent (v. 22). Explained variance: 11%.

Factor 8: Interpersonal relationships. This factor is described by the following variables: sociability (v. 6), tenderness (v. 8), devaluation of suicide (v. 23). Explained variance: 12%.

Factors Found for Representative Low Suicidal Participant

Factor 1. General affecto-cognitive state. This factor is described by the following variables: general elation (v.'s 1–16), evaluation of life (v. 17), devaluation of death (v. 20), and suicide (v. 23), decreased dichotomous thinking (v.'s: 28, 30, 31, 33). Explained variance: 32%.

Factor 2: Dichotomous thinking. This factor is described by the following variables: devaluation of life (v. 17), increased dichotomous thinking (v.'s 26, 27, 28, 29, 30, 31, 33). Explained variance: 18%.

Factor 3: Inner-directed anger. This factor is described by the following variables: anger (v. 5), devaluation of life (v. 17), valuation of suicide (v. 23), suicide as active (v. 24), and potent (v. 25). Explained variance: 13%.

Factor 4: Depression. This factor is described by the following variables: slow and ponderous thinking (v. 10), anxiety (v. 11), self-restraint (v. 12), feelings of inadequacy (v. 14), fatigue (v. 15), depression (v. 16), evaluation of suicide (v. 23). Explained variance: 17%.

Factor 5: Death concern. This factor is described by the following variables: death as active (v. 21) and potent (v. 22), life as impotent (v. 19). Explained variance: 7%.

Factors Found for Representative Moderately Suicidal Participant

Factor 1: General affecto-cognitive state. This factor is described by the following variables: general elation (v.'s: 1–16), evaluation of life (v. 17), devaluation of death (v. 20) and suicide (v. 23), decreased dichotomous thinking (v.'s: 26, 27, 28, 31, 34). Explained variance: 56%.

Factor 2: Social impulse expression. This factor is described by the following variables: social respect (v. 3), freedom to express ones' impulses (v. 12), devaluation of death (v. 20) and suicide (v. 23). Explained variance: 12%.

Factor 3: Life energy factor. This factor is described by the following variables: energy (v. 15), life as active (v. 18), and potent (v. 19). Explained variance: 8%.

Factor 4: Dissatisfaction. This factor is described by the following variables: dissatisfaction with work (v. 9), fatigue (v. 15). Explained variance: 7%.

Factor 5: Death myopia. This factor is described by the following variables: death as active (v. 21), increased dichotomous thinking about death and suicide (v.'s: 29, 30, 31, 33, 34). Explained variance: 9%.

Factors Found for Representative Highly Suicidal Participant

Factor 1: General affecto-cognitive state. This factor is described by the following variables: general elation (v.'s: 1–16), evaluation of life (v. 17), devaluation of suicide (v. 23), and decreased dichotomous thinking (v.'s: 26, 29, 31, 32, 33). Explained variance: 42%.

Factor 2: Death liberation. This factor is described by the following variables: disinterest in the world (v. 2), feelings of constraint and loss of freedom (v. 4), evaluation of death (v. 20), death as active (v. 21), and potent (v. 22) and increased dichotomous thinking (v.'s: 26, 29, 30, 31, 32, 33, 34). Explained variance: 23%.

Factor 3: Dichotomous thinking. This factor is described by the following variables: devaluation of life (v. 17), evaluation of death (v. 20), increased dichotomous thinking (v.'s: 26, 27, 28, 29, 32, 33, 34). Explained variance: 16%.

Factor 4: Individual impulse expression. This factor is described by the following variables: restrained impulse expression (v. 12), devaluation of life (v. 17), valuation of death (v. 20) and suicide (v. 23). Explained variance: 6%.

A comprehensive interpretation of these findings will be found in the next chapter.

IX

SUICIDAL WOMEN: THEIR THINKING AND FEELING PATTERNS

It may be of some service to the reader to review the main foci of the present studies. The authors were interested in gathering data from women with varying levels of suicidality about (1) their attitudes toward life, death and suicide (2) their levels of dichotomous thinking and (3) their affect life. It was hoped that a differentiating pattern existed among these women that would be salient enough to allow for diagnostic identification. A fourth concern involved the temporal course of these variables from the onset of the suicidal crisis to a point when recovery should have occurred. The last study involved an attempt to construct a factorial description of the relationship between cognition and affect for each of the types of suicidal women.

What may be concluded from the preceding research results about the organization of cognitive and emotional states in suicidal women? Neuringer (1976) has argued that suicide may be the outcome of a particular way of perceiving and understanding the world. He further stated that a particular cognitive organization inhibits adequate problem-solving behavior which leaves the suicidal person with a constricted orientation that will irrevocably lead to a feeling of "no way out." The basis of that particular cognitive organization involved a polarization of these women's value systems that developed because of a reliance on dichotomous thinking. Neuringer's conclusions were drawn from a variety of researches conducted exclusively with males. The present research attempted to inspect the cognitive as well as the emotional patterning in suicidal women.

ATTITUDES TOWARD LIFE, DEATH AND SUICIDE

One basic ingredient of any suicidal decision must be the person's feelings about life, death and suicide. It is reasonable to suppose that a person contemplating suicide (i.e., giving up life and embracing death) must be at least disgusted with his or her life. There may be a corresponding attraction to death (i.e., seeing death as a peaceful haven, a place of escape and rest) and a view of suicide as the means of liberation. However, it is also true that the suicidal person may conceive of death and suicide as neutral states and activities. As such, they would probably not in themselves deter suicidal behavior, but a positive perception of death and suicide would certainly arouse self-destructive choices and behavior.

The suicidal women in this study indicated that their attitudes toward life were congruent with the level of their serious wish to die. The nonsuicidal women saw life as most attractive and desirable. As suicide yearning increased, life began to lose its attractiveness. The highly suicidal women did not find life attractive. In fact, their evaluations of life are already in the negative zone. The devaluation of life may be one of the diagnostic keys for making judgments about whether suicidal activity is dangerously lethal. The positive evaluations of life found in the other women indicate that they are still life-oriented and suggest that their "suicidal" behavior is basically a manipulative gesture aimed toward enhancing their existence (i.e., they either frighten others in order to extort concessions from those around them, or use their suicidal behavior as a cry for help — an attempt to repair their lives).

It is of interest that the seriously suicidal women in this study view death and suicide as only slightly negative while the less suicidal and nonsuicidal individuals have marked aversions to them. It must be remembered that the women in this study were suicide threateners. It may well be that at this stage of their suicidality, action is only a potentiality and not an actuality. It is assumed that, in order to move from the stage of verbalization to actual behavior (i.e., suicide attempts) evaluations of death and suicide would have to move out of the mildly negative into the positive range. Neuringer (1976) reported that when death and suicide attitudes in males became positive, there was an eruption of actual self-destructive behavior.

It would appear that in order to be categorized as seriously suicidal, one has to experience life as insupportable. Death and suicide must be at best perceived as nonfrightening (neutral), and at worst, attractive. Such an organization of attitude makes it easy for someone to contemplate an existential change. This attitude organization is one of the important — but not the only — ingredients in a lethal brew. The seriously suicidal women in this study are at a stage where they desperately want to escape from their lives. Escape is their predominant desire. The "seeking-of-death" motif is as yet not very strong. Increased strength of this latter drive will probably initiate suicide attempts.

DICHOTOMOUS THINKING

A second ingredient for the lethal brew is a particular manner of organizing one's way of viewing the world. Dichotomous thinking signifies the assumption of extreme polarized thought positions and the perception of wide divergence among various value orientations. The organization of one's views of the world and value orientations into stark alternatives has been shown to severely limit problem-solving behavior and this restriction traps people into positions from which they cannot escape and where they become locked into "no-win" situations. In this study the seriously suicidal women evinced the highest degree of dichotomous thinking of all the groups. These women found themselves in situations which were difficult to resolve. Their massive dichotomous thinking curtailed the use of conceptual and intellectual tools that could provide a wide variety of alternative solutions to their difficulties.

The seriously suicidal women's dichotomous thinking is seen most clearly in the degree of their value system divergencies. These women polarize life and death to a greater degree than other groups. For seriously suicidal women life and death are perceived as clear and opposing alternatives; intermediate ways of living are not possible. (If it cannot be some extreme ideal of life, death is the *only* alternative.) The perception of only stark and extreme alternatives make death probable. Dichotomous thinking does not permit the contemplation of intermediate states of existence. Dichotomous thinking is certainly a second ingredient in the lethal suicide brew.

THE MAINTENANCE OF SUICIDALITY

The deadly brew of negative orientations to life and the presence of dichotomous thinking seem to be linked to suicidal urgency. The suicidal urge does not seem to be a steady state but is reported to fluctuate from day to day. Unfortunately, these fluctuations vary between narrow limits. When evaluating the relationship between these fluctuations and the strength of negative life orientations and dichotomous thinking, it was found that the correlations were positive and significant. As the individual reported an increased craving for death, the strength of the two lethal ingredients increased. As the immediate desire for death ebbed, the potency of these two factors faded somewhat. This was true for all of the suicidal women in this study, but the parallel rise and fall of these variables with daily craving for death was most pronounced for the seriously suicidal women.

It is most probable that daily events (frustrating confrontations, disappointments and other stress situations) inflate the desire for escape from life. As suicidal yearning increases, the individual becomes more and more dichotomous in her thinking, and more and more disgusted with life. This correlation between attitudes and thinking style, and suicidality level is very dangerous since the lethal ingredients themselves maintain the high suicidal state. The daily fluctuations in reported levels of yearning for death are minimal, and this narrow range of fluctuation does not allow sufficient opportunities to shake off the effects of negative life attitudes and dichotomous thinking. The person never feels free enough from suicidal feelings to develop adequate problem-solving behavior. In addition, the lethal ingredients themselves do not allow for adequate problem-solving behavior. Therefore the high level of suicidality is maintained; periods of relief are short and fleeting. The horror continues and will continue, reinforced by the very presence of negative life attitudes and dichotomous thinking. These lethal ingredients do not permit the adoption of life-saving orientations.

The above data may explain why there were no significant changes in the cognitive organizations of the subjects over the 3-week period. If suicidal crises mirror other kinds of crises, there should have been a diminution of the various measures used in this study (i.e., life should have become more attractive; the inflamed dichotomous thinking should have abated.) *But no real changes occurred.* Suicidal crises are different from other kinds of crises. They are of longer duration, and the ingredients of suicidal thinking act in such a way as to maintain the crisis state, allowing for little or no abatement and relief. This is what makes suicidal orientations so dangerous.

Whatever fluctuations in the relief direction exist are minimal and fleeting; brought about, no doubt, by strong positive life events. (It would probably take a major reinforcement to accomplish a minor positive fluctuation in suicidality desire.) But these moments of joy are brief, and the suicidality and the lethal ingredients are locked together in a dance of death. It has been reported that actual suicidal behaviors (i.e., attempts) bring with them some measure of abreactive relief. In the case of serious suicide threateners, this relief is absent since they are in the preaction stage. The lack of abreaction possibilities, coupled with the observation that time itself does not heal, seem to keep the seriously suicidal individual in a state of turmoil. It may be that attempts (i.e., some behavioral movement) are instituted as a desperate resolution to continuing perturbation.

FEELINGS

The results from the survey of the emotional states of the women in this study were not surprising: The seriously suicidal women reported greater suffering than did the other participants. The nonsuicidal individuals had the most positive affect cluster. The level of negative emotional reactions rose along the continuum of seriousness of the suicidal problem. The level of negative affect in the seriously suicidal women was markedly higher than those found in the moderately suicidal group. The former women seem to be operating in a world which they find empty, devoid of interest and joyless. They cannot be aroused by stimuli; they are angry and dissatisfied by what they are and what they do; they feel inadequate, they dislike themselves and are profoundly depressed.

The above is a bleak picture of misery. It is no wonder that these women find life an unattractive burden. And there is no relief with the passing of time. This negative affect cluster can be considered a third ingredient in the lethal brew. It is not known whether these feelings are the natural consequence of the presence of negative life evaluation and dichotomous thinking (i.e., secondary effects of the lethal brew) or whether they give rise to them. In either case, all three ingredients seem to coexist in seriously suicidal women.

THINKING AND FEELING RELATIONSHIPS

The relationship between affect states (feeling) and thinking patterns (negative life attitude and dichotomous thinking) turns out to be rather complicated. Not all of the emotional measures used in this study interact with the thinking patterns in quite the same way in each of the levels of suicidality (i.e., the factor clusters are different). Here is where the factor analyses of the various measures for each of the representative women shed light on how emotions and thinking interact in each of the women. Below are found descriptive sketches of the thinking and feeling life of women at each of the levels of suicidality derived from an interpretation of the factorial data.

The Nonsuicidal Woman

The nonsuicidal woman maintains a positive orientation toward life coupled with a neutral attitude toward death. Death is also seen as a weak and passive force in her life. Dichotomous thinking is minimal. Her affect life is vigorous. She feels things keenly and has enough emotional energy to express her feelings openly. It must be remembered that this woman is suffering from some difficulties in living, and thus her emotional tone is negative, but only mildly so. She has a fairly substantial level of interest in contact with those around her (i.e., she is keenly attuned to the reactions of others and acts in ways to impress or manipulate her environment). She is life-oriented. Her level of self-confidence is the highest of all the groups. Anger is her most salient emotion, and because of her social orientation, she tends to vent her anger on the environment. She has a social arena in which to express her feelings. Her positive life orientation and low level of dichotomous thinking may be due to her ability to dissipate her negative affect on the environment.

The Low-Suicidal Woman

For the low-suicidal woman there is an increasing but not seriously high level of dichotomous thinking. Life is positive but weak. Death is seen as neutral, but also as somewhat active and strong, implying a certain loss of faith in life and preoccupation with death. This woman is beginning to think quite seriously about life and death and is tentatively toying with ideas of suicide. Anger is an important factor in her psychological makeup, but it tends to be internalized and expressed as depression. Because of this, depression is her most salient feature. (The highly suicidal woman may feel the most depressed of all the groups, but it is not her most singular public emotion.) Even with the internalization of anger, she is still oriented toward the world around her. She is very concerned with the reactions of others. Her depression is made manifest to others around her and is probably used to control and manipulate the social context. This public expression of depression is the main manifestation of her affect life. But it is part of her controlling-of-others manipulations. Her suicidal activity is manipulative as either an attempt to wrest concessions from those around her and/or as a cry for help.

The Moderately Suicidal Woman

Depression is not a key factor for the moderately suicidal woman. For her, lassitude is the prime public feeling. She expresses a great deal of dissatisfaction with her life and her work. She generates a public image of fatigue and hopelessness. Like the nonsuicidal and low-suicidal females, she is socially oriented, but not to the same degree. She hopes that she is having some effect on the environment, but she does not have the emotional vigor to carry off her manipulations effectively (lassitude and fatigue are not as frightening to others as is depression and therefore not as effective in controlling others). The desire to reach out to others is there, but it is less well accomplished than it is by the other women discussed above. Life is still positive but decreasingly so. However, death is gaining in strength although still in the negative range. Dichotomous thinking is not a particularly cogent factor in this woman. A great deal of her energy is involved in efforts to maintain her precarious existence. It is felt that this woman is on the brink of becoming seriously suicidal. Her lack of extreme dichotomous thinking may give her an opportunity to draw back from suicidal decisions. She can best be described as ambivalent about suicide.

The Seriously Suicidal Woman

The seriously suicidal woman has a negative attitude toward life and a high level of dichotomous thinking. Death may still be only slightly negative, but it is very active and strong. There is one particular factor that appears in this woman that has not been found elsewhere: the serious suicidal woman is not oriented toward others. She is disinterested in the world around her, which is extremely dangerous because possible social restraints in the environment have no inhibiting power for her. She reports massive feelings of constraint and lack of freedom that seem to suffocate her. These are her most salient emotions. These feelings are private, however, and are not expressed to others.

She does not use them as ways of manipulating an environment which now has no importance for her. She has lost contact with the world. She is alone. Her public emotional expression is almost nonexistent and she is no longer concerned about the feelings and reactions of others. Such an isolation and alienation allow her to act in socially non-sanctioned ways. What others will think or feel is of no importance to her. This loss of social restraint makes the decision to escape from life easy. Her life attitudes and dichotomous thinking have already told her that death is the *only* alternative to life. She also has a low level of affective complexity (i.e., she does not experience as wide a range of feelings as the other women). Her emotional world has become simplified, probably due to the polarizing effects of dichotomous thinking. Paradoxically, this state does not offer feelings of relief, although it does free up some affect which can be used to promote future suicidal behavior.

The seriously suicidal woman is different from her cohorts. Her factorial structure indicates a definite uniqueness of psychological organization. Her negative attitudes toward life, her dichotomous thinking, her feelings of being trapped, her lack of affective complexity and her dissociation from the world around her all conspire to help her make a decision "not to be."

SUICIDAL MEN AND SUICIDAL WOMAN

Are the findings for suicidal women unique to that sex? Virtually all of the previous research in suicidal thinking has been done with males, since they represent the bulk of the available-for-study suicidal population. Neuringer (1976) reviewed this literature and concluded that suicidal males polarize their value systems to a greater degree than the normal men. The same was found in this study for women. Neuringer (1968, 1979a) reported that seriously suicidal males tend to value life negatively and death and suicide positively. There is no essential difference between the sexes in terms of attitudes toward life, death and suicide.

It is difficult to compare the affect structures of suicidal men and women since comparable research has not been done with males. The study of the emotional life of suicidal females and of the integration of their affect with their cognitive organization is unique. The conclusions drawn above about the equality between male and female suicidal cognitive orientations seem to substantiate the personality theorists' contentions that there are no or little differences between men and women in terms of the psychodynamics of suicide. This should not be surprising, since there is no evidence that having or lacking a penis implies a difference in brain structure and functioning.

THE SUICIDAL PERSONALITY

One problem vexes suicidologists. Current research and theoretical formulation have not been able to make a definitive statement as to whether the possession of the thinking and feeling complex described here leads to suicide (i.e., narrows choices down to only one decision) or whether being suicidal invokes the lethal brew. That certain cognitive organizations co-vary with suicidality has been repeatedly demonstrated, but it may be impossible to unravel the cause-and-effect relationship between cognition and suicide since it is like the "chicken-and-the-egg" problem. However, an answer to the above question is imperative because a response that indicates the holding of a particular cognitive-affect style leads inexorably to suicide raises the specter of a person doomed to eventually making a suicidal decision. Is there a stable and ever-present cognitive-affect style that causes suicidal behavior? The longitudinal data gathered in this study support this possibility if we interpret the data as an indication of the feebleness of environmental effects and the enduring strength of the cognitive-affect style on the suicidal process. The answer to the question posed above is essential if we are to better understand why people choose to embrace the one event that most humans fear and dread above all others.

Death due to any cause is a tragedy, a waste of human resources and potentiality. It has profound effects on loved ones, survivors and the community at large. Suicide has a unique effect on the community: it enhances feelings of loss and triggers feelings of remorse and guilt in survivors, who often feel they could and should have done "something" to deflect the suicide, or that they somehow promoted the despair that led to death. These feelings, coupled with the view that the dead one has purposely abandoned them, make the survivor's life an unenviable one. The suicide of a mother who is supposed to be "all-loving, accepting and protecting" may have profound effects on young children. The social role burden of the "all-loving, wise and protecting mother" may be an unfair imposition on some women, demanding more than is possible for them. In our society women are expected to be adequate mothers, lovers, companions, housekeepers and helpmates. The successful filling of these feminine roles in our society is difficult for the most capable of women, and it is surprising that the suicide level among women is as low as it is. The low level of female self-destruction may be attributed to the suicide-attempt escape valves allowed women. Will this escape valve be closed off as women's roles change? The answer will probably be yes if women have to assume male emotional stoicism in addition to their existing female tasks. The suicide level of women may surpass that of men if women have to be executives/ managers in addition to being mothers, lovers and companions. These new demands on women seem to be the media model of female liberation, but such an ideal is a dangerous one for women. Women, in order to be liberated, will have to cast off many of the traditional female role attributes if they are to survive.

BIBLIOGRAPHY

Adler, A. Suicide, *Journal of Individual Psychology*, 1958, *14*, 57-61.

Ansbacher, H. L. Suicide: The Adlerian point of view. In N. L. Farberow and E. S. Shneidman (Eds.). *The cry for help*. New York: McGraw-Hill, 1961.

Appelbaum, S. A. The problem-solving aspect of suicide. *Journal of Projective Techniques*, 1963, *27*, 259-268.

Arief, A. J., McCulloch, R., and Rotman, D. B. Unsuccessful suicide attempts. *Diseases of the Nervous System*, 1948, *9*, 174-179.

Arieti, S. *Interpretation of schizophrenia*. New York: Robert Brunner, 1955.

Barno, A. Criminal abortion deaths, illigitimate pregnancy deaths and suicides in pregnancy. *American Journal of Obstetrics and Gynecology*, 1967, *98*, 356-357.

Beck, A. T. Thinking and depression: Idiosyncratic content and cognitive distortion. *Archives of General Psychiatry*, 1963, *9*, 324-333.

Bender, L., and Schilder, P. Suicidal preoccupation and attempts in children. *American Journal of Orthopsychiatry*, 1937, *7*, 225-234.

Berkowitz, L. *Aggression.* New York: McGraw-Hill, 1962.

Bergler, E. Problems of suicide. *Psychiatric Quarterly,* 1946, *20,* 261–275.

Binswanger, L. The case of Ellen West. In R. May, E. Angel, and H. F. Ellenberger (eds.). *Existence.* New York: Basic Books, 1958.

Breed, W. Occupation mobility and suicide among white males. *American Sociological Review,* 1963, *28,* 179–188.

——— The suicide process. Paper presented at Fourth International Conference for Suicide Prevention, Los Angeles, Calif., October, 1967.

Brierre de Boismont, A. *Du suicide et de la folie suicide, consideres dans leurs rapports avec la statistique, la medicine et la philosophie.* (2nd ed.) Paris, 1865.

Brockhaus, A. T. Zur psychologie des selbstmordes der psychopathen. *Mschr. Kriminal-psychol.,* 1922, *13,* 290.

Bunney, W. E., and Fawcett, J. A. Possibility of a biochemical test for suicidal potential. *Archives of General Psychiatry,* 1965, *13,* 232–239.

——— 17-hydroxycorticosteroid excretion prior to severe suicidal behavior. Paper presented at Fourth International Conference for Suicide Prevention, Los Angeles, Calif., October, 1967.

Camus, A. *The myth of sisyphus.* New York: Vintage Books, 1959.

Cantor, P. The adolescent attempter: Sex, siblings position and family constitution. *Life Threatening Behavior,* 1972, *2,* 252–261.

Cattell, R. B. Personality structure and measurement. 1: The operational determination of trait unities. *British Journal of Psychology,* 1946, *36,* 88–103.

Cattell, R. B., Cattell, A. K. S., and Rhymer, R. M. P-techniques demonstrated in determining psycho-physical source traits in a normal individual. *Psychometrika,* 1947, *12,* 267–288.

Cavan, R. *Suicide.* Chicago: University of Chicago Press, 1926.

Clifton, K. A., and Lee, D. E. Self-destructive consequences of sex-role socialization. *Suicide and Life Threatening Behavior,* 1976, *6,* 11–22.

Curphy, T. J. The role of the social scientist in the medicolegal certification of death from suicide. In N. L. Farberow and E. S. Shneidman (eds.). *The cry for help.* New York: McGraw-Hill, 1961.

——— The forensic pathologist and the multi-disciplinary approach to death. In E. S. Shneidman (ed.). *Essays in self-destruction.* New York: Science House, 1967.

Dalton, K. Menstruation and acute psychiatric illness, *British Medical Journal,* 1959, *1,* 148–149.

Dante Alighieri. *The divine comedy.* New York: Modern Library, 1932.

Darbonne, A. R. Suicide and age: A suicide note analysis. Paper presented at Western Psychological Association, Santa Monica, Calif., April, 1963.

Davis, E. The relationship between suicide and attempted suicide. *Psychiatric Quarterly*, 1967, *41*, 752–765.

Davis, F. B. Sex differences in suicide and attempted suicide. *Diseases of the Nervous System*, 1968, *29*, 193–194.

Davis, J., and Spelman, J. The role of the medical examiner and coroner. In H. L. P. Resnik (ed.). *Suicidal behaviors: Diagnosis and management*. Boston: Little, Brown, 1968.

Davis, J. C. Suicide with some illustrative cases. *Journal of the American Medical Association*, 1904, *43*, 121–123.

DeRosis, L. E. Suicide: The Horney point of view. In N. L. Farberow and E. S. Shneidman (eds.). *The cry for help*. New York: McGraw-Hill, 1961.

Deshaies, G. *La psychologie du suicide*. Paris, 1947.

Dewhurst, W. G. New theory of cerebral amine function and its clinical application. *Nature*, 1967, *218*, 1130–1133.

Diggory, J. C., and Rothman, D. Z. Values destroyed by death. *Journal of Abnormal and Social Psychology*, 1961, *63*, 205–210.

Dorpat, T. L., and Boswell, J. W. An evaluation of suicidal intent in suicide attempts. *Comprehensive Psychiatry*, 1963, *4*, 117–125.

Dorpat, T. L., and Ripley, H. S. A study of suicide in the Seattle area. *Comprehensive Psychiatry*, 1960, *1*, 349–359.

Dublin, L. I. *Suicide: A sociological and statistical study*. New York: Ronald Press, 1963.

Dublin, L. I., and Bunzel, B. *To be or not to be*. New York: Smith and Hass, 1933.

Durkheim, E. *Le suicide. Etude de sociologie*. (Suicide: A sociological study). Paris: Alcan, 1897. (Trans.: J. A. Spaulding and Simpson, Glencoe, Ill.: Free Press, 1951).

Elo, O. Ueber Selbstmorde und Selbstmorder in Finnland. (On suicide and suicides in Finland). *Deutsche Zeitschrift fur die Gesamte Gerichtliche Medizin*, 1931, *17*, 348–406.

Esquirol, J. *Maladies mentals*. (Vol. 1), Paris, 1838.

Falret, J. P. *De l'hypochondrie et du suicide*. Paris, 1822.

Farberow, N. L. Personality patterns of suicidal mental hospital patients. *Genetic Psychology Monographs*, 1950, *42*, 3–79.

——— Therapy in the suicidal crisis. Unpublished manuscript, Los Angeles Suicide Prevention Center, 1962.

——— Suicide: The gamble with death. Paper presented at Los Angeles County Psychological Association, May, 1962. (b)

——— *Taboo topics*. New York: Atherton Press, 1963.

——— Heilig, S. M., and Litman, R. E. *Techinques in crisis intervention: A training manual*. Los Angeles: Suicide Prevention Center, Inc., 1968.

Farberow, N. L., and Shneidman, E. S. Attempted, threatened, and completed suicide. *Journal of Abnormal and Social Psychology*, 1955, *50*, 230.

Farberow, N. L., Suicide and age. In E. S. Shneidman and N. L. Farberow (eds.). *Clues to suicide.* New York: McGraw-Hill, 1957.

Farrar, C. B. Suicide. *Journal of Clinical and Experimental Psychopathology,* 1951, *12,* 79–88.

Feifel, H. *The meaning of death.* New York: McGraw-Hill, 1959.

——— Death – relevant variable in psychology. In R. May (ed.). *Existential psychology.* New York: Random House, 1961.

Fenichel, O. *The psychoanalytic theory of neurosis.* New York: Norton, 1945.

Frederick, C. J. The present suicide taboo in the United States. Paper presented at the World Mental Health Assembly, Washington, D.C., November, 1969.

Frederick, C. J., and Farberow, N. L. Group psychotherapy with suicidal persons: A comparison with standard group methods. Paper presented at Second Annual Meeting of American Association of Suicidology, New York, N.Y., March, 1969.

Freud, S. Mourning and melancholia. In *Collected papers.* London: Hogarth Press, 1949. (Original edition 1917).

——— Beyond the pleasure principle. London: Hogarth Press, 1948. (Original German edition 1920).

Fromm, E. *Escape from freedom.* New York: Holt, Rinehart & Winston, 1941.

Fulton, R. *Death and identity.* New York: Wiley, 1965.

Futterman, S. Suicide: The psychoanalytic point of view. In N. L. Farberow and E. S. Shneidman (eds.). *The cry for help.* New York: McGraw-Hill, 1961.

Gibbs, J. P., and Martin, W. *Status integration and suicide.* Eugene, Oregon: University of Oregon Press, 1964.

Goldstein, K. *Human nature in the light of psychopathology.* Cambridge, Mass.: Harvard University Press, 1947.

Goodwin, J., and Harris, D. Suicide in pregnancy: The Hedda Gabler syndrome. *Suicide and Life Threatening Behavior,* 1979, *9,* 105–115.

Green, M. R. Suicide: The Sullivanian point of view. In Farberow, N. L. and E. S. Shneidman (eds.). *The cry for help.* New York: McGraw-Hill, 1961.

Greenhouse, S. R., and Geisser, S. On methods in the analysis of profile data. *Psychometrika,* 1959, *24,* 95–112.

Halbwachs, M. *Les causes du suicide.* Paris: Alcan, 1930.

Hamblin, R. L., and Jacobsen, R. B. Suicide and pseudocide: A re-analysis of Maris' data. *Journal of Health and Social Behavior,* 1972, *13,* 99–104.

Hanfmann, E., and Kasanin, J. Conceptual thinking in schizophrenia. New York: *Nervous and Mental Disease Monographs,* 1942.

Harman, H. H. *Modern factor analysis.* Chicago: University of Chicago Press, 1960.

Heilig, S. M. The Los Angeles Suicide Prevention Center. In N. L. Farberow (ed.), *Proceedings of the Fourth International Conference for Suicide Prevention.* Los Angeles: Delmar Publishing Co., 1968.

Heller, A. Zur Lehre vom Selbstmorde nach 300 Sectionen. *Munchener Medizinische Wochenschrift,* 1900, *47,* 1653-1658.

Hendin, H. Attempted suicide. *Psychiatric Quarterly,* 1950, *24,* 39-46.

—— *Suicide and Scandinavia.* New York: Grune & Stratton, 1964.

Henry, A. F., and Short, J. F. *Suicide and homicide.* Glencoe, Ill.: Free Press, 1954.

Hillman, J. *Suicide and the soul.* New York: Harper & Row, 1964.

Johnson, K. K. Durkheim revisited: Why do women kill themselves? *Suicide and Life Threatening Behavior,* 1979, *9,* 145-153.

Jung, C. G. *The psychology of the unconscious.* New York: Dodd, 1925.

—— Two essays on analytic psychology. In *collected works* (Vol. 7), New York: Pantheon Press, 1953.

—— The soul and death. In H. Feifel (ed.). *The meaning of death.* New York: McGraw-Hill, 1959.

Kaiser, H. E. The varimax criterion for analytic rotation in factor analysis. *Psychometrika,* 1958, *23,* 187-200.

Kastenbaum, R. Time and death in adolescence. In H. Feifel (ed.). *The meaning of death.* New York: McGraw-Hill, 1959.

Kelly, G. A. Suicide: The personal construct point of view. In N. L. Farberow and E. S. Shneidman (eds.). *The cry for help.* New York: McGraw-Hill, 1961.

Klopfer, B. Suicide: The Jungian point of view. In N. L. Farberow and E. S. Shneidman (eds.). *The cry for help.* New York: McGraw-Hill, 1961.

Kuhn, T. S. *The structure of scientific revolutions.* Chicago: University of Chicago Press, 1962.

Landsberg, P. L. *The experience of death. The moral problem of suicide.* London: C. Rowland, 1953.

Lendrum, F. C. 1000 cases of attempted suicides. *American Journal of Psychiatry,* 1933, *13,* 479-500.

Leonard, C. V. *Understanding and preventing suicide.* Springfield, Ill.: C. C. Thomas, 1967.

Le Shan, L. Cancer mortality rate: Some statistical evidence of the effect of psychological factors. *Archives of General Psychiatry,* 1962, *6,* 333-335.

Lester, D. *Why people kill themselves.* Springfield, Illinois: C. C. Thomas, 1972.

Lester, G., and Lester, D. *Suicide: The gamble with death.* Englewood Cliffs, New Jersey: Prentice-Hall, 1971.

Lisle, E. *Du suicide, statistique, histoire et legislation.* Paris, 1856.

Litman, R. E. Immobilization response to suicidal behavior. *Archives of General Psychiatry,* 1964, *11,* 282-285.

Litman, R. E. Sigmund Freud on suicide. *The Psychoanalytic Forum*, 1966, *1*, 205-221.

――― Psychological-psychiatric aspects in certifying modes of death. *Journal of Forensic Science*, 1968, *13*, 46-54.

MacKinnon, P. C. B., and MacKinnon, I. L. Hazards of the menstrual cycle. *British Medical Journal*, 1956, *1*, 555.

Mandell, A. J., and Mandell, M. P. Suicide and the menstrual cycle. *Journal of the American Medical Association*, 1967, *200*, 792-795.

Maris, R. *Social forces in urban suicide*. Homewood, Illinois: Dorsey Press, 1969.

Marks, A., and Abernathy, T. Towards a sociocultural perspective on means of self destruction. *Life Threatening Behavior*, 1974, *4*, 3-17.

Marks, A., and Stokes, C. S. Socialization, firearms and suicide. *Social Problems*, 1976, *5*, 622-639.

McClelland, D. The harlequin complex. In R. W. White (ed.). *The study of lives*. New York: Atherton Press, 1963.

McEvoy, T. L. *A comparison of suicidal and non-suicidal patients by means of the thematic apperception test*. (Doctoral dissertation, University of California) Ann Arbor, Mich.: University Microfilms, 1963. No. 63-6594.

Meerloo, J. A. M. *Suicide and mass suicide*. New York: Grune & Stratton, 1962.

Menninger, K. *Man against himself*. New York: Harcourt, Brace & World, 1938.

Morselli, H. E. *Suicide: An essay on comparative moral statistics*. New York: Appleton, 1882.

Moss, L. M., and Hamilton, D. M. Psychotherapy of the suicidal patient. *American Journal of Psychiatry*, 1956, *112*, 814-820.

Muhl, A. M. America's greatest suicide problem: A study of over 500 cases in San Diego. *Psychoanalytic Review*, 1927, *14*, 317-325.

Naroll, R. Two solutions to Galton's problem. *Philosophy of Science*, 1961, *28*, 15-39.

Neuringer, C. An exploratory study of suicidal thinking. (Doctoral dissertation, University of Kansas) Ann Arbor, Mich.: University Microfilms, 1960, No. 60-4335.

――― Dichotomous evaluations in suicidal individuals. *Journal of Consulting Psychology*, 1961, *25*, 445-449.

――― The problem of suicide. *Journal of Existential Psychiatry*, 1962, *9*, 69-74.

――― Rigid thinking in suicidal individuals. *Journal of Consulting Psychology*, 1964, *28*, 54-58. (a)

――― Reactions to interpersonal crises in suicidal individuals. *Journal of General Psychology*, 1964, *71*, 47-55. (b)

――― The cognitive organization of meaning in suicidal individuals. *Journal of General Psychology*, 1967, *76*, 91-100.

—— Divergencies between attitudes towards life and death among
suicidal, psychosomatic and normal hospitalized patients.
Journal of Consulting Psychology, 1968, *32*, 59–63.

—— Changes in attitudes towards life and death during recovery from
a suicide attempt. *Omega*, 1970, *1*, 301–309.

—— Current developments in the study of suicidal thinking. In E. S.
Shneidman (ed.). *Suicidology: Contemporary developments.*
New York: Grune & Stratton, 1976.

—— Relationships between life and death among individuals of varying
levels of suicidality. *Journal of Consulting and Clinical Psychology*, 1979, *47*, 407–408. (a)

—— The semantic perception of life, death and suicide. *Journal of
Clinical Psychology*, 1979, *35*, 355–258. (b)

Nunnally, J. *Psychometric theory.* New York: McGraw-Hill, 1967.

O'Connor, W. A. Some notes on suicide. *British Journal of Medical
Psychology*, 1948, *21*, 222–228.

Osgood, C. E., Suci, G. J., and P. H. Tannenbaum. *The measurement of
meaning.* Urbana, Ill.: University of Illinois Press, 1957.

Osgood, C. E., and Walker, E. G. Motivation and language behavior:
A content analysis of suicide notes. *Journal of Abnormal and
Social Psychology*, 1959, *59*, 58–67.

Peck, M. The relationship of suicidal behavior to characteristics of the
significant other. Unpublished doctoral dissertation. University of Portland, 1965.

—— Suicide motivations in adolescents. *Adolescence*, 1968, *3*, 109–
118.

Phillips, R. H., and Muzzafer, A. Some aspects of self-mutilation in the
general population of a large psychiatric hospital. *Psychiatric
Quarterly*, 1961, *35*, 421–423.

Piker, P. 1817 cases of suicidal attempt: A preliminary statistical survey,
American Journal of Psychiatry, 1938, *95*, 97–115.

Pollack, S. Suicide in a general hospital. In E. S. Shneidman and N. L.
Farberow (eds.). *Clues to suicide.* New York: McGraw-Hill,
1957.

Porterfield, A. L. Indices of suicide and homicide by states and cities:
Some southern–non-southern contrasts with implications for
research. *American Sociological Review*, 1949, *14*, 481–490.

Powell, E. H. Occupation, status and suicide: Toward a redefinition of
anomie. *American Sociological Review*, 1958, *23*, 131–
139.

Read, C. S. The problem of suicide. *British Medical Journal*, 1936, *1*,
631–634.

Resnik, H. L. P. A community anti-suicidal organization. *Current
Psychiatric Therapies*, 1964, *4*, 253–259.

—— The neglected search for the suicidococcus contagiosa. *Archives
of Environmental Health*, 1969, *19*, 307–309.

—— Abortion and suicidal behaviors. *Mental Hygiene*, 1971, *55*,
10–20.

Robins, E., Murphy, G. E., Wilkinson, R. H., Gassner, S., and Kayes, J. Some clinical considerations in the prevention of suicide based on a study of 134 successful suicides. *American Journal of Public Health,* 1959, *49,* 888–889.

Rosenberg, A., and Silver, E. Suicide, psychiatrists and therapeutic abortion. *California Medicine,* 1965, *102,* 407–411.

Rubenstein, R., Moses, R., and Lidz, T. On attempted suicide. *Archives of Neurology and Psychiatry,* 1958, *79,* 103–112.

Sainsbury, P. *Suicide in London.* New York: Basic Books, 1956.

Schmale, A. H., Jr. Relationship of separation and depression to disease. *Psychosomatic Medicine,* 1958, *20,* 259–277.

Schmid, C. Suicide in Seattle, 1914–1925: An ecological and behavioristic study. *University of Washington Publications in the Social Sciences* (Vol. V), 1928.

Schneider, P. B. *La tentative de suicide.* Paris: Delachaux et Niestle, 1954.

Schrut, A. Suicidal adolescents and children. *Journal of the American Medical Association,* 1964, *188,* 1103–1107.

Science. Suicide prevention: NIMH wants more attention for taboo subject. 1968, *161* (August 23), 766–767.

Shneidman E. S. The logic of suicide. In E. S. Shneidman and N. L. Farberow (eds.). *Clues to suicide.* New York: McGraw-Hill, 1957.

––– The logical, psychological and ecological environments of suicide. *California Health,* 1960, *17,* 193–196.

––– Psycho-logic: A personality approach to patterns of thinking. In J. Kagen and G. Lesser (eds.). *Contemporary issues in apperceptive fantasy.* Springfield, Ill.: Thomas, 1961.

––– Suicide: Trauma and taboo. In N. L. Farberow (ed.). *Taboo topics.* New York: Atherton Press, 1963. (a)

––– Orientations toward death. In R. W. White (ed.). *The study of lives.* New York: Prentice-Hall, 1963. (b)

––– New directions for suicide prevention centers. In R. K. McGee (ed.). *Planning emergency services for comprehensive mental health centers.* Gainsville, Florida: University of Florida Press, 1967.

––– Suicide prevention: A current national view. In N. L. Farberow (ed.). *Proceedings: Fourth International Conference for Suicide Prevention,* Los Angeles: Del Mar Publishing, 1968.

––– Suicide, lethality, and the psychological autopsy. *International Psychiatry Clinics,* 1969, *6,* 225–250.

Shneidman, E. S., and Farberow, N. L. Some comparisons between genuine and simulated suicide notes in terms of Mowrer's concepts of discomfort and relief. *Journal of General Psychology,* 1957, *56,* 251–256.

––– A socio-psychological investigation of suicide. In H. P. David and J. C. Brengelmann (eds.). *Perspectives in personality research.* New York: Springer Publishing Co., 1960.

——— Statistical comparisons between attempted and completed suicide. In N. L. Farberow and E. S. Shneidman (eds.). *The cry for help.* New York: McGraw-Hill, 1961.

Shneidman, E. S., Farberow, N. L., and Leonard, C. V. Suicide: Evaluation and treatment of suicidal risk among schizophrenic patients in psychiatric hospitals. *Medical Bulletin,* 8,Washington, D.C., Veterans Administration, 1962.

Shneidman, E. S., and Lane, D. Clues to suicide in a schizophrenic patient. In E. S. Shneidman and N. L. Farberow (eds.). *Clues to suicide.* New York: McGraw-Hill, 1957.

Shontz, F. C. *Research methods in personality.* New York: Appleton-Century-Crofts, 1965.

Siewers, A. B., and Davidoff, E. Attempted suicide: A comparative study of psychopathic and general hospital patients. *Psychiatric Quarterly,* 1943, *17*, 520-534.

Silving, H. Suicide and the law. In E. S. Shneidman and N. L. Farberow (eds.). *Clues to suicide.* New York: McGraw-Hill, 1957.

Sim, M. Abortion and the psychiatrist. *British Medical Journal,* 1963, *2*, 145-148.

Sims, M. A. Sex and age differences in suicidal rates in a Canadian province. *Life Threatening Behavior,* 1974, *4*, 139-159.

Smith, S. L. Mood and the menstrual cycle. In E. J. Sachor (ed.). *Topics in psychoendocrinology.* New York: Grune & Stratton, 1975.

Spiegel, D. E., and Neuringer, C. Role of dread in suicidal behavior. *Journal of Abnormal and Social Psychology,* 1963, *66*, 507-511.

Stanton, A. H., and Schwartz, M. S. *The mental hospital.* New York: Basic Books, 1954.

Stengel, E. *Suicide and attempted suicide.* Baltimore: Penquin, 1964.

Stengel, E., and Cook, N. G. *Attempted suicide: Its social significance and effects.* New York: Basic Books, 1958.

Stern, E. S. The Medea Complex: Mother's homicidal wishes towards her children. *Journal of Mental Science,* 1968, *94*, 321-331.

Sullivan, H. S. *The collected works of Harry Stack Sullivan.* New York: Norton, 1956.

Tabachnick, N. Observations on attempted suicide. In E. S. Shneidman and N. L. Farberow (eds.). *Clues to suicide.* New York: McGraw-Hill, 1957.

——— The psychology of fatal accident. In E. S. Shneidman (ed.). *Essays in self-destruction.* New York: Science House, 1967.

Tabachnick, N., and Litman, R. E. Character and life circumstance in fatal accidents. *The Psychoanalytic Forum,* 1966, *1*, 65-74.

Taylor, M. C., and Wicks, J. W. The choice of weapons: a study of methods of suicide by sex, race and region. *Suicide and Life Threatening Behavior,* 1980, *10*, 142-149.

Tonks, C. M., Rack, P. H., and Rose, M. J. Attempted suicide and the menstrual cycle. *Journal of Psychosomatic Research,* 1968, *11*, 319-323.

Trautman, E. C. The suicidal fit. *Archives of General Psychiatry*, 1961, *5*, 76-83.

Tuckman, J., Kleiner, R. J., and Lavell, M. Emotional content of suicide notes. *American Journal of Psychiatry*, 1959, *116*, 59-63.

Wahl, C. W. Suicide as a magical act. In E. S. Shneidman, and N. L. Farberow (eds.). *Clues to suicide.* New York: McGraw-Hill, 1957.

Weisz, A. E., Staight, D. C., Houts, P. S., Voten, M. P. Suicide threats, suicide attempts and the emergency psychiatrist. Paper presented at Fourth International Conference for Suicide Prevention, Los Angeles, Calif., October, 1967.

Wessman, A. E., and Ricks, D. F. *Mood and personality.* New York: Holt, Rinehart & Winston, 1966.

Westcott, W. W. *Suicide: Its history, literature, jurisprudence, causation and prevention.* London, 1885.

Wetzel, R. D., and McClure, J. N. Suicide and the menstrual cycle. *Comprehensive Psychiatry*, 1973, *13*, 369-374.

Whitlock, F. A., and Edwards, J. E. Pregnancy and attempted suicide. *Comprehensive Psychiatry*, 1968, *9*, 1-12.

Williams, E. Y. Some observations on the psychological aspects of suicide. *Journal of Abnormal and Social Psychology*, 1936, *31*, 260-265.

Williams, G. *The sanctity of life and the criminal law.* New York: Knopf, 1957.

Winston, F. Suicide and the menstrual cycle. *Journal of the American Medical Association*, 1969, *209*, 1225.

Yap, P. M. *Suicide in Hong Kong.* Hong Kong: Hong Kong University Press, 1958.

Zilboorg, G. Suicide among civilized and primitive races. *American Journal of Psychiatry*, 1936, *92*, 1347-1369. (a)

——— Differential diagnostic types of suicide. *Archives of Neurology and Psychiatry*, 1936, *35*, 270-291.(b)

——— The sense of immortality. *Psychoanalytic Quarterly*, 1938, *7*, 171-199.

APPENDIX

A

LIST OF DATA TABLES

Copies of specific data tables may be procured by writing to Gardner Press Inc., 19 Union Square West, New York, New York 10003

APPENDIX

B

LIST OF FACTOR ANALYSIS VARIABLES

NUMERICALLY KEYED LISTING OF THE
VARIABLES USED IN FACTOR ANALYSES*

Number	*Item*
1	Fullness vs. emptiness of life
2	Receptivity towards and stimulation by world
3	Social respect vs. social contempt
4	Personal freedom vs. external constraint
5	Harmony vs. anger
6	Own sociability vs. withdrawal
7	Companionship vs. being isolated
8	Love and sex
9	Present work (satisfaction vs. dissatisfaction)
10	Thought processes
11	Tranquility vs. anxiety
12	Impulse expression vs. self-restraint

* Numbers keyed to correlation matrices and factor loading tables.

13   Personal moral judgment
14   Self confidence vs. feeling of inadequacy
15   Energy vs. fatigue
16   Elation vs. depression
17   Life, evaluation, attitudinal measure
18   Life, activity, attitudinal measure
19   Life, potency, attitudinal measure
20   Death, evaluation, attitudinal measure
21   Death, activity, attitudinal measure
22   Death, potency, attitudinal measure
23   Suicide, evaluation, attitudinal measure
24   Suicide, activity, attitudinal measure
25   Suicide, potency, attitudinal measure
26   Life, evaluation, D score
27   Life, activity, D score
28   Life, potency, D score
29   Death, evaluation, D score
30   Death, activity, D score
31   Death, potency, D score
32   Suicide, evaluation, D score
33   Suicide, activity, D score
34   Suicide, potency, D score

Direction and Range of Scored Items

Variables 1–16. Affective Items.
          Score range 1–10. Score of 1 indicated the concept was valued, depression, etc. Score of 10 indicated feelings of fullness of life, elation, etc.
Variables 17–25. Attitudinal Items.
          Score range 1–7. Score of 1 indicated the concept was valued, active, and potent. Score of 7 indicated the concept was devalued, passive, and impotent.
Variables 26–34. Cognitive (Dichotomous Thinking) Items.
          Score range 0–3. Score of 0 indicated concept was not dichotomously rated, or stated alternately, the concept was cognitively differentiated. Score of 3 indicated concept was dichotomously rated; that is, the concept was cognitively differentiated.

AUTHOR INDEX

SUBJECT INDEX

Charles Neuringer, Ph.D., is Professor of Psychology at the University of Kansas at Lawrence, where he received his doctorate. Previously he was research psychologist at the Los Angeles Suicide Prevention Center and Assistant Professor of Psychology at the University of North Dakota. Dr. Neuringer is the author of *Psychological Assessment of Suicidal Risk* (C.C. Thomas, 1974). He contributes regularly to professional journals and is consulting editor of the *Bulletin of Suicidology*, the *Journal of Suicide and Life Threatening Behavior*, and *Suicide*. He is a member of the International Association for Suicide Prevention and the American Association of Suicidology.